T0369294

THE THREE-WORD

TRUTH

ABOUT LOVE

AND

BEING WELL

THE THREE-WORD

TRUTH

ABOUT LOVE

AND

BEING WELL

***

A

TESTAMENT

Order this book online at www.trafford.com
or email orders@trafford.com

Most Trafford titles are also available at major online book retailers.

© Copyright 2009 Clark Falconer.
Editor: Anita Chakrabarti
All rights reserved. No part of this publication may be reproduced, stored in a retrieval
system, or transmitted, in any form or by any means, electronic, mechanical, photocopying,
recording, or otherwise, without the written prior permission of the author.

Note for Librarians: A cataloguing record for this book is available from Library
and Archives Canada at www.collectionscanada.ca/amicus/index-e.html

Printed in Victoria, BC, Canada.

ISBN: 978-1-4251-7607-5 (softcover)
ISBN: 978-1-4251-7608-2 (e-book)

*We at Trafford believe that it is the responsibility of us all, as both individuals
and corporations, to make choices that are environmentally and socially sound.
You, in turn, are supporting this responsible conduct each time you purchase a
Trafford book, or make use of our publishing services. To find out how you are
helping, please visit www.trafford.com/responsiblepublishing.html*

*Our mission is to efficiently provide the world's finest, most comprehensive
book publishing service, enabling every author to experience success.
To find out how to publish your book, your way, and have it available
worldwide, visit us online at www.trafford.com*

Trafford rev. 6/1/2009

 www.trafford.com

North America & international
toll-free: 1 888 232 4444 (USA & Canada)
phone: 250 383 6864 ✦ fax: 250 383 6804 ✦ email: info@trafford.com

The United Kingdom & Europe
phone: +44 (0)1865 487 395 ✦ local rate: 0845 230 9601
facsimile: +44 (0)1865 481 507 ✦ email: info.uk@trafford.com

10 9 8 7 6 5 4 3 2 1

Testament: a commitment to show that something exists and is true.

Contents

PROLOGUE

Through your decision to open this book you are falling into a life-enriching process.

As you read, do not seek immediate understanding. This book is meant to be experienced; understanding will follow later. Expect surprising and sometimes confusing feelings and reactions that will have a powerful effect on you. You will feel afraid. Let yourself flow into the words. You are falling into LOVE.

Opening gently with WON'T, the text shapes into WILL and reaches fullness in the depth of AM.

Each WORD is Introduced and its Principles outlined.

The Practice is carefully guided and the Source and Process revealed.

Then in truth, THREE WORDS come together in a field of LOVE.

Afterwards LOVE'S ESSENCE is explored.

INTRODUCTION

We know for certain now that the way we think changes everything. Our words are sources of light and energy, darkness and pain and, as soon as we think something it begins to happen.

Yet most people stay stuck in lower consciousness. They don't tap into the vast energy available to them in higher consciousness simply because they misunderstand and misuse words and their associated feelings.

Most people can see and feel the power of words that circulate in their minds but they have in effect lost their minds because their words, as below, run on in endless bursts and circles of negativity fed by feelings of lower consciousness.

Negative Thought: I am repulsive.
Lower Consciousness Feeling: Anxiety.
Negative Thought: I am repulsive.

Negative Thought: My pain is unbearable.
Lower Consciousness Feeling: Depression.
Negative Thought: My pain is unbearable

This book outlines a simple process that shows you how to effectively take back your mind and well-being by harnessing the incredible energy of LOVE through the power in THREE WORDS.

SEEING AND KNOWING

As you become comfortable with the THREE WORDS, you will be developing your until-now-latent, spiritual faculty of **seeing**, the uncanny sensation and feeling of **knowing** something with absolute, intuitive conviction.

Knowing in turn will be developing and evolving. This is the powerful, eerie certainty of understanding something with absolute, intuitive conviction.

Intuitive **knowing** is the pre-rational immediate awareness of the wholeness of experience and existence. There is no cloud over this **seeing** and **knowing**; this is feeling and certainty beyond doubt.

Now keeping these ideas in mind, consider that you have divided yourself into one part called your untrue-self and another called your true self.

THE UNTRUE SELF

The untrue-self is your very real, very necessary, self-and-other-created surface. It is secondary and made up of a diversity of consciousnesses.

The untrue-self sees a world made up of separate parts. It includes a self-important, unique part you think of as 'me' alone. This 'me' is distinct from 'I' in relation to others in the world.

Your untrue-self terrorizes by threatening the loss of your stuff, your body, your physical health, your relationships, your individuality and your country. It operates both consciously and unconsciously. It is constructive in aiding growth, development and survival and destructive in hiding your true self and the essences of LOVE.

Your untrue-self 'me', in fearing relationship with others, attacks 'I' in order for learning to take place. If the necessary learning fails to take place, your awareness is consumed by LOVE.

The addictions of all kinds, worrying and other self-destructive behavior such as violence to self or others, over-concern about and need for pleasure, fears of disease or bodily imperfection, avoiding pain, controlling others, perfectionism, dwelling in guilt-based-care-taking, suffering, fame, money and power are features of your untrue-self.

Cause and effect achievements in the material world are constructive features of your untrue-self.

THE TRUE SELF

Your true self, to the contrary, is real, not created, both a part of, and in, the whole world. It is your primary core and perfect background presence of 'I' in relationship to other.

Your true self has no limits. It lacks nothing.

Your true self contains a single point of immense energy and unified consciousness with others. It fully accepts pain, disability and the miracle of death, yet rejects all illness, disease and suffering.

The wisdom of the true self from the deep often seems bafflingly inconsistent with the surface purposes of the untrue-self.

The true self operates in the best interests and well-being of 'I' but seems monstrously threatening because of the ease with which it can devour everything, including lower consciousness awareness, in the infinite energy of LOVE.

Both your untrue-self and true self can be pictured as distinct from each other and as different as black and white, life and death, day and night, but these two selves are in reality one: the greater-or-lesser-integrated-self in its relationship to the world.

Your untrue-self is a fence around nothing. Your true self is complete awareness held safely by the THREE WORD filaments of LOVE, it **sees** and **knows** the unity of all.

IMAGINING

Imagine.

Imagine the single word CALM.

Imagine this word in the center of your mind.

Hold this image in the center of your mind and slowly let it fill your whole mind and body.

Now imagine that this one word, filling you with CALM, can change your life, because it can.

Keep your eyes closed and imagine the word CALM again in the center of your mind.

Now let the word CALM be replaced by the word UNTRUE-SELF.

Now picture the word, TRUE SELF.

Now imagine these two selves coming together in your mind, in truth, in one word: LOVE.

Hold the word LOVE there.

Now open your eyes.

Watch how your world is beginning to change color and texture, everything brighter, softer.

You are slowly falling into LOVE and being well.

Don't try to make sense of this according to your past schemas. Remember, you are transforming into the mystery of your life in LOVE.

THE THREE WORDS

The THREE WORDS take you to your true self to remind you that you are already here. Together they are information of being well, pointing you to the only energetic reality: the experience and awareness of LOVE.

In the experience and practice below you are about to rediscover the qualities of your inner being and acquire the necessary knowledge to regain, with transcending intuitive awareness, your life and innocence, the miracle of your death and being well.

WORD ONE: You discover the most Empowering Knowledge of WON'T.

WORD TWO: You discover the Advanced Creative Knowledge of WILL.

WORD THREE: You discover Eternal, Infinite Being in the unified spirit of AM.

> No should.
> No have to
> No ought to.
> No can't.
> No I'm not able.

No I don't know.
No I'll try.
No I don't remember.
No hidden meanings.

You are on the threshold of new and profound experiences.
You are daring to become increasingly aware.

You are about to feel deeply what you are and what the world is when you fall into LOVE.

You will doubt.
You will become excited.
You will feel irritated.
You will feel intensely angry.
You will feel afraid.

But now simply open up to the THREE WORDS and gently fall back, back, into your memory of LOVE.

WON'T, WILL and AM: THREE WORDS revealing two levels of Knowledge, a third level of Being Well and the miracle of receptive spirit that waits in LOVE.

WON'T

We begin with the story of a man and woman.

DANNY AND SARAH

DANNY

Mr. Danny Quill is a dutiful son and a dedicated father. He phones his mother every day and travels across town to visit her every Friday for lunch. He works hard at his job with the government, as a planner. He hasn't made a successful plan for years.

Early in his career Danny excitedly put together ideas that created a lot of buzz around the office, but none of his ideas were taken to completion and lately he feels completely uninspired. He still goes to the odd meeting to make his presence known. He reads memos that cross his desk almost every day. He knows in advance they are going to be about how the names of departments are changing, or, that there are other big changes coming.

Danny lost his idealism years ago. He fights every day now to overcome his apathy and not become completely cynical. He has been at this job too long to expect anything to happen. He has learned that as long as he keeps his head down they probably won't bother him. Still, the job is security for his family and he makes a decent fixed income.

Danny has little left over from his check every two weeks and he spends hours at work obsessing about how he can make more money. Not the kind of guy who is willing to kiss up, he knows he has no hope of, or even desire for, advancement. He has dental, three weeks holiday a year, good disability health coverage and twenty years invested in the company pension plan. The benefits are very important to him. On many an occasion, after a couple of beers with his colleagues, he has been known to say, 'I'll need the benefits, this job is killing me.'

Danny has been drinking more and more for the last fifteen years. While he has had one DUI, he has never lost his license and he still feels his drinking is under control. He switched to expensive vodka last year. He has been taking a sleeping pill, now sometimes two, for several years. Danny still doesn't sleep well so he often tops up his pills with a toke of marijuana that he sneaks out on the back deck to smoke before he goes to bed.

Sometimes when he can't sleep, Danny slips out to his tool-shed to admire his latest toy. Each toy is a purchase from the huge box hardware store that he often finds himself aimlessly wandering around in after work. He always smiles at the irony of the joke, the guy who dies with the most toys wins, because he feels like he is dying and he knows he is not winning.

His shed is so full of toys he can barely fit in another one. He trembles at the thought of his wife discovering he is waiting delivery on a new ATV for deer hunting. He felt he just had to have this new machine, but he also knows he caved to the sales pitch and bought it impulsively.

Danny and his wife started sleeping in separate beds three years ago because she tossed and turned and he snored. He used Viagra for a while, because he was having problems, but now they have had no sex life for two years. He has lately found himself getting aroused by dwelling on porn websites at work.

Danny and Sarah don't fight much anymore to protect the children.

After worship on the weekend they often go for a visit he dreads, to see Sarah's ill mother in the rest home. His boys refuse to go anymore but he feels a peculiar, powerful obligation to elders.

SARAH

Mrs. Sarah Quill is a stay-at-home mother who has dedicated her life to her three sons 18, 16 and, her 'baby', 11. She worries her oldest has a drug problem because his grades are slipping. He often skips school.

Sarah is worried her 16 year old is depressed and took him to a psychiatrist where he was put on antidepressants. This resulted in his becoming suicidal, taking an overdose, and being admitted to a psychiatric ward.

Sarah is always exhausted and to get through the day she has started smoking again. She secretly shops during the day for the latest fashions on-line, hiding them from her husband. She drinks two pots of coffee before noon.

Sarah has finally got her weight down to under a hundred pounds. She ballooned to over two hundred pounds again, for the third time, during her last pregnancy. She still thinks she is too fat and nothing she buys on-line fits her, so she ends up hiding her latest purchases in the basement laundry room.

Sarah has lost touch with most of her friends except her neighbor and coffee pal, Linda, who has a significant weight problem. Linda thinks she is patiently leading Sarah to the light and the way, but she really helps Sarah feel better by simply lending an ear. Unbeknownst to Linda her presence on the one hand helps Sarah feel slimmer, but on the other hand makes Sarah feel worse, as Linda is a mirror of Sarah's distorted image of herself.

Sarah still lies down beside her 'baby' at night and sings him lull-a-byes, often ending up falling asleep in his bed. When she makes it to her own bed she often wakes up to find 'baby' sleeping with her. To her consternation he still pulls his hair and bites his nails. She is very worried he might be gay as she caught him wearing her panties.

Sarah talks to her mother at least three times a day on the phone but her mother seldom makes sense anymore. Sarah always hangs up feeling guilty that she doesn't visit her more often.

Sarah finds herself thinking more and more about her first boyfriend, Martin, who was perfect and got away. He dumped her after getting accepted into medical school.

Often Sarah spends the day in bed with a headache or her fibro acting up. She reads romance novels, or, falls asleep in the midst of a fantasy during her afternoon soap.

Sarah seldom goes out now except to see her family doctor to get a refill of Valium. Sometimes she is still in bed when Danny and the children come home from school and work. This creates a lot of tension, as everyone is hungry.

Sarah feels she is completely out of ideas for what to make for dinner and the thought of shopping for food or cooking again makes her want to slash her wrists.

Sarah wonders if she has attention deficit disorder and should be on Ritalin, but her doctor, so far, has refused to prescribe it.

* * *

Spend a moment asking yourself if you can see any part of yourself anywhere in this story.

Before you begin your life transformation below, review the above story and think about Mr. and Mrs. Quill's well-being and why they are not in LOVE.

WON'T

The Pure Conscious Knowledge of What I WON'T Do in the Local Material World.

Introduction

Your FIRST WORD, WON'T, and your first sentence, I WON'T, while giving an immediate impression of negativity, is the beginning of a renewed feeling of ease and elation, a sense of eternal life wherein labor is eliminated but not action nor activity.

Living your life fully in the FIRST WORD, and facing the demands of everyday life, it will feel as if you have to resist, that to say I WON'T will be too great an effort. It will seem difficult to understand fully how it works.

But keep in mind that initially understanding how WON'T works is not necessary. You are investing in non-doing because you have decided you want absolutely everything, including well-being and that beyond understanding: LOVE.

You will first focus on the outer world and develop necessary skills of self-discipline. You will move on to shape your inner world by highlighting your own interior experience.

Before you read this testament, to be healthy and sane meant to stay locked in fixed patterns of living. As you change these patterns inside, in your thoughts and feelings, and outside in your behavior, you may be looked upon as eccentric, insane or deranged.

Be assured that in WON'T you haven't lost your mind; all you are losing is your fixed habit patterns. As you let go of these patterns, and keep your feet on the ground, you will live an incredibly richer, stronger, abundant life. You are coming to **know** that to change your habits of thinking, feeling and behaving is the beginning of being well and embracing, and being embraced by, LOVE.

It will be a struggle. The more sensitive you are the more vulnerable you will feel. You will be tempted by old ways of making sense of life by changing nothing and getting more of the same.

WON'T defines who you are by simply stating, without excuse or complaint, without explanation, the things you will not do. With WON'T in place you begin to experience the beauty of truth.

WON'T is forgiving yourself and others for errors, learning the presented lessons, and then letting go of all personal history. Contrary to social indoctrination, being true to your self is more important than any group loyalty.

WON'T has incredible fear, shame, envy and guilt attached to it in your unconscious body and mind where phantom monsters from the past hide. You learn from your past to plan your future, but you keep in mind the past's biggest lesson: Do not dwell where nothing exists.

WON'T you **see** is always up against most potent enemies: negative emotions, negative thoughts and self-destructive behavior. Your untrue-self attacks your true self and others, living in fear of thoughts, feelings, actions and reactions that WON'T brings to the surface.

Nothing will test WON'T, the development of your new system of living, more than dealing with impossible people in positions of power. As you still take them personally and seriously, you will thereby feel you have nothing to fall back on.

All bullies, internal and external, whether frightened, angry, disabled, or deformed, are unknowingly teachers of LOVE. The bully is the mirror of your inner world, the outside world you can't control, someone who holds power, or someone who simply annoys you to distraction.

What helps you is **seeing** that know-it-alls are better for you the more their character is repugnant. Bullies offer you exactly what you need: the opportunity to say I WON'T and thereby not get caught up in self-importance.

When you face situations with tranquility by saying I WON'T to every rush of feeling tempting you to act madly, you acquire the centeredness and peace of mind to face the unknown and then even the unknowable. You work on having no points to defend, to be perfectly flexible, but rigidly clear about WON'T.

As you practice WON'T, you will soon discover and then begin to feel, significant shifts in the rhythm and flow of your internal energy. This internal work transforms how you **see** yourself, others and the world you live in. You stop taking care of others.

WON'T is the foundation for all that follows, making your life an end in itself free of words except where you choose them for their informational and energetic usefulness and effectiveness.

The real secret is that you can no more bypass the necessity of WON'T than you can bypass the truth and beauty of death.

The pure consciousness of WON'T arises in the instant of acceptance of the miracle of death. Now you learn to hold dearly to new **knowledge**: WON'T faces and dissolves all fear and negativity. You begin to shape your life of being well in LOVE.

In the next phases of this process you will find pure, positive answers and the unfolding of enlightened personal development. But, without the seeming negative WON'T, the amazing transformation to bliss and peace of mind in WILL and AM is not possible.

Nothing can be attracted to your life unless through WON'T you commit to repulsing all toxic negativity from your external world and commit to letting go of all toxins in your heart.

You will still experience the untrue-self, raw fear of being cast off, lonely and impoverished, but, as you become comfortable with the phrase I WON'T, you pan through the gravel of all negativity and glimpse the gold nuggets of your calm, true-self emerging.

The Principles of WON'T

☐ WON'T is letting go. Feeling alive begins with what you refuse.

☐ WON'T is not clinging. All except essentials are expendable.

☐ WON'T is not judging. Judgment arises from interacting cartoon images in your mind.

☐ WON'T is forgiveness. All is fully forgiven.

☐ WON'T is the end of criticism, blame, attack, gossip, justification and defending.

☐ WON'T is refusal to identify with your body. This is where fear, shame, envy, guilt, vanity, suffering and illness reside.

☐ WON'T is validation and letting go of the lower consciousness feelings, fear, anger, envy, regret, resentment and guilt and their accompanying habitual thoughts and behavior.

☐ WON'T is facing the reality of external or internal danger.

☐ WON'T is freedom from being right. Polarization of your life and single points of view are let go.

☐ WON'T is strengthening your moral sense, but only at the behest of LOVE.

☐ WON'T is not complaining or explaining. There is nothing you have to do.

☐ WON'T is letting go of all personal history.

As these 12 aspects of WON'T become centered in your consciousness with full awareness, you begin the giant leaps to I WON'T believe in illness, I WON'T believe in disease, I WON'T believe in suffering and then to approach the truth that I WON'T be ill and I WON'T suffer.

The SOURCE and PROCESS of WON'T

LOVE is the source of WON'T, infusing it to moderate temptation, impulses and addictive cravings. Letting go of regrets, resentments, blame and fear is the empowerment of WON'T.

The Birth of WON'T

In order to put the energetic word WON'T into perspective think back to the source of your birth. Think of the growth of a baby from a fertilized ovum.

This is internal growth. It is distinct from external, social, or political growth where, like a building, the whole is constructed from the outside.

Out of the amniotic fluid of parental imperfection to a greater or lesser extent life inevitably begins as a trial with too much or too little love in some combination. This most vital human gift of love is then distorted by exposure to all kinds of negative feelings, thoughts and behavior.

So you enter a process in a human form, wanting what you want when you want it, quickly coming up against innumerable obstructions and frustrations.

Yours was a miraculous journey through the birth canal, from breathing amniotic fluid to gasping for air. Your umbilical cord was cut with scissors. You cried with hunger pangs. Your mouth sought a more or less ready to feed breast. You attained motor control and began to sit, speak and then walk. Thus you faced innumerable challenges, satisfactions and frustrations of your material form, your untrue-self development first crystallizing in the interactive reality of toilet training.

External forces, social and parental, demanded you do something and, as a child, you struggled to be in charge of internal forces and material. This was the necessary separation into subject and object, matter from self.

The proverbial battle of the chamber pot began where a distorted I WON'T begins, often degenerating into the evil twin, I can't, and ending up decades later in protests, politics and power struggles of all kinds. The relentless march to triumph, control, contempt, fame, power, fortune, marital strife, murder, war and unconsciousness are all examples of this means to unending suffering.

WON'T in Society

The ordering of your mind and body, as complex as the ordering of the stars, takes on, through social and then personal installation, a simplistic series of roles that unite at a social level but divide at a personal one: husband, wife, student, dentist, mayor, bus driver, politician, used car salesman, social worker, etc, etc. You are taught, and necessarily, unconsciously agree, to be something, and the price tag is your freedom.

Your untrue-self is necessarily separated from your true self in the battle with others in your mind and in society. Your true self rejects the social installation of thoughts of who you are, thoughts in turn savored by the growing power of your untrue-self. And equally your true self rejects control, while your untrue-self uses social power to control and direct your behavior.

The resultant ignorance about, and estrangement from, your true self, explains your feelings of emptiness and isolation. This is your all too continuous, unsettling sense of living vicariously rather than experiencing the blissful reality of the energy field of LOVE you are. Thus reared to act untruly, without stopping to feel, the distorted, malignant growth of self-denigration, defensiveness and self-importance begins.

These roles, chosen almost solely for personal power and enslavement of others, lead to your enslavement, as they inflate and deflate your untrue-self. At the same time they undermine your sense of reality and sense of connection to what you know from the whispers of your heart and body: your true self speaking to you of LOVE.

I WON'T is therefore remarkably simple, but not easy, because, in a metaphoric and real sense, it is building a new way of **seeing** the relationship with society and your whole world. In order to begin to **see** you need to validate your past, but at the same time cut the chains to memory's emotions: emotions that give you the illusion of being solid.

To the degree you are still playing boss you are holding back and resisting what your true self **knows**. You are thinking and believing that your old comfortable patterns of misery and suffering are where you'd rather be. You are out in society unconsciously deciding to give into fear, anger, envy and guilt with I can't.

But now, you will almost imperceptibly become so comfortable in saying I WON'T, that you will be able to avoid struggle completely. You will accept responses from others whatever their level of consciousness.

You doubt I WON'T because this exacting practice requires you to give yourself totally over to transformation. You face your enormous longing to be taken care of, your fear of social isolation, impoverishment and loneliness, your fear of being shunned and criticized. You keep in mind that your true self is primarily revealed in what you oppose.

The Wisdom of WON'T

Wise women and men, understanding the source of the true self, often respond with a version of I WON'T when asked to speak about enlightenment, or the way, or the path. When they feel interested to respond, say out of love for a student, they often speak in riddles, koans, or parables, or give a reply such as: 'The answer is in not doing.'

These teachers recognize that thought must be silent if it is to reveal its source, follow its own movement, and think about anything other than itself. They know that words follow to and from thought, words about words, leading to the fantasy that the word, usefully classifying Nature, is prior to Nature itself.

In fact, the wise fully understand that energetic words are much more importantly a creative, informational radiance that flows out of LOVE from the natural true self mind.

These teachers also know that the true self mind, the source of information, energy, and purpose, is hidden within by unconsciously created fixed patterns of thought and feeling based on past experiences. They **see** that this untrue-self mind creates a misleading dual reality, a world of false safety, fear, conflict and self-doubt separating it from your true self, mind and body.

Your silent, but wide-open mind, revealed by WON'T, is free of narrow, linked, untrue-self dualities. It no longer separates experience from the one experiencing. It is the center point of one consciousness in your true self.

The world is now a seamless unity of interdependent relationships. It is not something you form a relationship with, but something with which you have an intrinsic relationship.

Everything is intelligible only in terms of relationships held together by LOVE. In organic order, the whole is primary and parts arise mutually within it.

Now through WON'T you begin to **see** that subject and object are not really separate. You **see** that spirit and matter are one.

WON'T in LOVE

Lovers say I WON'T. They don't live in the past or fear the future. They understand intuitively, for instance, that activities like making and saving money, preparing to live, confusing counting and measuring with reality, come with the high cost of not being alive in the moment.

Closer and closer to falling into LOVE, trying to express their intense, blissful feelings for their beloved, they struggle with unity consciousness. They feel blocked by the uselessness of words when their attempt to overcome separateness in 'I love you' seems so hopelessly inadequate.

They only partially understand that love between forms is finite, while LOVE is its own meaning, and this meaning itself is only freed by fully accessing WON'T.

The true self when freed by WON'T, moves through life with rhythm and no preconceived course of action or taboo. It decides for each moment what the right thing is to do, expressing and experiencing the essence of inherent human-heartedness, loving the world and being in LOVE.

WON'T frees compassion, gratitude, peace and quiet. Its energy radiates out to others inviting them to live in this place of neutrality and calm acceptance. You grow into LOVE in WON'T by allowing the world to be and loving it.

You are no longer a person who acts solely on your own but a process that is free to say I WON'T. This is **seeing** that all is blessed and from this blessing you drink and bathe in life's warm, thirst-quenching moisture. You feast, without a trace of greed, on an infinite supply of LOVE.

Now you **see** a world of creativity and spontaneity beyond pain and suffering, free of cycles of negativity, buoyed by growing, interdependent love.

Fully in the process of WON'T, you let go of memories and living in the past. You let go of fears, desires, hopes and expectations of the future. You begin to live, completely taken care of, fully alive in the present, tapped into the infinite energy of LOVE.

The Process of WON'T

It is shocking at first to go more deeply, to experience fully the joy and energy awaiting you when you **see** you **know** absolutely nothing and that what you think you know is self-and-other-created illusion.

Start to watch carefully how much of your perception of the real world is based on gossip, complaining, negativity and the sale of fear. These poisons prey on your need for false security making it seem impossible to say I WON'T.

Without WON'T, seemingly inexplicably, your material stuff becomes a bigger and bigger pile, a heavier and heavier anchor around your poor, aching, bending neck. Others give you stuff, heavy stuff; they call on you to see your new stuff and to show off theirs.

But, your consciousness, through WON'T, transforms into the realization of the illusion of suffering, the illusion of illness and disorder that you alone create. You begin to let go.

In saying I WON'T, your growing awareness unmasks and then removes all power from the fear and self-absorption in the coffin of your self-denigration and self-importance, revealing the miracle of death itself. You are opening up a gap, getting ready to transcend life and death.

Now deeply in the process of WON'T, repeat I WON'T to yourself silently so you begin to know, feel, sense and experience your single purpose. At first your attention will collapse easily. You will want to fall asleep, to get moving, to do something, or you will engage in internal gossip so as to not aim and sustain your attention on WON'T.

Each time your attention collapses forgive yourself. Watch and witness the thoughts, the sensations and the feelings that divert you. **Know** these experiences, recognize their pattern, and return and embrace the principles and exercises of WON'T again and again with firm conviction and intention.

WON'T at first sounds harsh and cold and tough, rude and forceful. As you become comfortable with it, and **see** it is saying goodbye to all suffering, you **see** WON'T for what it is, soft, gentle, and at its source, incredibly empowering, peaceful and innocent, free of effortful control.

With WON'T you don't force and you aren't in a fight. You watch your surrender; a surrender that doesn't contain negativity like I don't care, or, I can't be bothered. WON'T is caring with your very life.

Dwell in the innocent and blameless, guilt-free world you are creating. Let the past go entirely, not worrying about the next second, **knowing** that all is unfolding perfectly.

There is nothing to fear. There is no reason for guilt. There is no mystery to be solved now, no strange incantations or meditations, just the repetition of a plain and simple word: WON'T.

You are innocent. Be completely insecure. This is where life exists at its fullest. Start to say it to yourself, introduce it into your relationship interactions. Each instant in WON'T transforms and elevates your consciousness.

WON'T embodies the essence of your blossoming life and points the way to infinity, eternity, freedom, being well and celestial bliss in LOVE. Focus on WON'T and go into it deeply.

Don't underestimate how hard it is going to be and how long it is going to take before you are ready to move on to the SECOND WORD: WILL. But also remember that your life begins its transformation into LOVE and being well the instant you **know** the power of WON'T.

THE PRACTICE OF WON'T

1) Practice with one exercise phrase for five minutes twice a day, morning and night, until you have completed the WON'T exercise phrases below.

2) There will accrue to you the immediate benefit of calming and centering your mind. You will notice and feel the long-term benefit of storing up well-being, clarity, calmness and centeredness energy.

3) Breathe in I WON'T, swallow I WON'T, see I WON'T, feel I WON'T and let the sound of the words resonate, vibrate and develop rhythm as they sink deeply into your body, every cell energizing and in turn being energized.

4) As you arise each day preparing for your exercise allow yourself to sink into the peace of WON'T by reminding yourself that initially saying I WON'T may sound like a temper tantrum. This will stimulate seeds of guilt in you and fear in those around you. They will, in turn, unconsciously be downloading guilt and anger on you in reality and in the images in your mind. They will say, "You can't say the words I WON'T, you can't even think the words I WON'T." This kind of response shows that those around you, in reality, and in your mind, are still living unconscious, guilt, shame, envy and fear-based lives.

5) WON'T, no matter how lovingly said, is a direct affront to all unconsciousness. It is the first invitation to wake up. Your acceptance and forgiveness of others is complete because you

understand that everyone is doing their best from their own level of conscious development.

6) Keep in mind as you do the exercise, that I WON'T is not just saying no to others, it is watching, witnessing and saying no to your own untrue-self impulses, feelings and thought patterns.

7) Watching your thoughts and feelings in WON'T, you will start to become aware of past patterns of grief, patterns of resentment and patterns of regret and mourning for your later contemplation. You will **see** these patterns trying to pull you back into unconsciousness.

8) You gently cast these anchors off and, filling with well-being, you catch the gentle breeze of LOVE and sail freely.

========================

WON'T Exercises

Record five minutes of calming, non-vocal music and use it as a source of relaxation and as a timer.

The exercise is best done in the same comfortable chair each time, as free as possible from discomfort and distraction. If necessary it can be repeated under any circumstances at any time.

Start your music and begin by sitting comfortably with your eyes closed.

Take a deep breath in and let it out slowly.

As you breathe out, let your whole body relax and stress dissolve.

Continue doing this for thirty seconds to center and calm your mind.

Keeping your eyes closed you begin your vital work with WON'T.

Begin by directing your attention to saying I WON'T and thus focusing on your internal life.

Repeat slowly while breathing in, "I WON'T" then breathing out, "indulge in self-pity. Count: One ".

Breathe in, "I WON'T", breathe out, "indulge in self-pity, two".

Breathe in, "I WON'T", breathe out, "indulge in self-pity, three".

Repeat this very slowly for ten sets.

When you reach ten focus on your breathing again and let any remaining stress flow from your body.

Now let the word LOVE fall back into the center of your mind. Breathe in LOVE and imagine your whole body and mind filled with well-being and LOVE.

Hold LOVE in the center of your mind. Let it fill your body until your music stops.

Now open your eyes.

You have begun to store up calmness and life energy. You return control of your mind to your true self by becoming clear about what you WON'T do.

Notice how the world seems more pleasant and not as sharp-edged.

==========================

WON'T examples for daily practice

I WON'T judge.

I WON'T indulge in greed.

I WON'T focus on weakness.

I WON'T attach to stuff.

I WON'T attach to outcomes.

I WON'T force or be forced.

I WON'T push to the front.

I WON'T have anything to defend.

I WON'T indulge in self-pity.

I WON'T indulge in self-importance.

I WON'T indulge in self-denigration.

I WON'T indulge in jealousy or envy.

I WON'T indulge in confusion, laziness or craziness.

I WON'T…. Below are five examples to help you start resolving your own personal struggles. Consider these typical situations where it would be in the best interest of your well-being to access WON'T.

While adding an item may seem simple, or even simplistic, if you want to live in LOVE and being well, remember the work involved requires dedicated, daily practice.

1) You are peacefully driving when you are suddenly cut off by another car. Your mind fills with rage and you find yourself

ruminating with violent and vengeful thoughts about this and other similar incidents. You are aware your anger has taken control of your mind. You wake yourself up and access WON'T. You add this new item to your practice list:

I WON'T be ruled by anger.

2) Your teenage son has borrowed your car and hasn't returned at the promised hour. You find yourself pacing with worry. You then become aware you have devoured a full bag of potato chips and two thick slices of chocolate cake. You go to bed feeling ill. You toss and turn, your mind racing with thoughts of catastrophe. You wake yourself up and access WON'T. You add this item to your practice list:

I WON'T live in worry and fear.

3) You get the good news you are getting money back on your taxes and the same afternoon you are told you are up for a raise and a promotion. You are elated. Without thinking, you go for one drink after work, but the next thing you know you find yourself inebriated in a casino. You wake yourself up and access WON'T. You add another item to your practice list:

I WON'T act self-destructively.

4) You have a fight with your boyfriend and he abruptly ends your relationship. You find yourself overwhelmed with sadness and anger, shaking with fear. The next thing you know you have spent the whole afternoon shopping. With your trunk full of purchases, you become aware you are speeding through traffic and cutting off other cars. You wake yourself up and access WON'T. You add this item to your practice list:

I WON'T be overwhelmed by my feelings.

5) A good friend hasn't kept a promise and isn't returning your call. You find yourself pacing your office with disappointment unable to focus on your work. You become aware you forgot to attend an important meeting. You wake yourself up and access WON'T. You add this item to your practice list:

I WON'T behave irresponsibly in response to others.

I WON'T --- now add the central issues you are working on.

Having completed this work, you are ready now to move onto the second WORD: WILL.

DANNY AND SARAH

Now imagine the Quill couple again as they contemplate the seemingly overwhelming tasks before each of them.

How hard will it seem to Danny to say I WON'T to his mother, his wife, his job, his need for security, his growing alcoholism, his wife's dependence on her family, his addictions, spending on toys, marijuana, sleeping pills and pornography?

How hard will it seem to Sarah to say I WON'T to her mother, her husband, her children, her friend, her vanity, her cigarettes, her fantasies of the regretted past, her indulgence in sleep, her sleeping with her eleven year old son, her worries about her son's sexuality, her addictions to Valium, coffee, online-shopping and her eating disorder?

When we consider the seeming magnitude of these tasks we are able to **see** the power that must first be accessed in WON'T to clear the slate. We also **see** the enormous fear of impoverishment, loneliness, sadness and longing that WON'T generates as the slate is cleared.

This is why the strength and reassuring presence of the SECOND WORD brings such important focus to our attention and intent. WILL shapes life out of seeming chaos and nothing.

WILL

DANNY AND SARAH

DANNY

As we arrive on the scene again, we approach difficult, seemingly impossible scenarios to even imagine. We see Danny has quit his deadening job, sold all his toys, cashed in his pension, rented a small apartment, began divorce proceedings from his wife, told his mother he will keep in touch but he won't be coming for lunch every Friday, quit marijuana cold, cancelled his internet contract and all of his insurance policies. He has also thrown away his sleeping pills. His boys still won't speak to him but he is sure they will come around. This sounds like a complete personal revolution and we wonder what is he going to do next?

SARAH

Sarah, while briefly considering thoughts of suicide and, shocked by Danny's leaving, soon after actually found she was surprisingly relieved. Forced to work, she took the first job she could find and told her oldest son, in no uncertain terms, he was going to have to pay room and board or move out. Sarah then told her middle son he had to get a part time job and contribute to the house. Lastly, she told her now 12- year-old son that sleeping with her was over and she meant it.

Sarah spoke with her neighbor Linda and told her she was too busy with her work and upgrading class in the evening to set aside any more time for coffee. Linda passively protested and promised to pray for her.

Sarah picked up her phone. After a couple of helpful crisis meetings with her psychiatrist, she excitedly settled on a new direction. Feeling strong enough, she cancelled her next appointments. She then threw away her Valium and cigarettes. Now we have a second personal revolt going on. What will Sarah do next?

*   *   *

Be assured, if Danny and Sarah are truly in revolt and want to be well and in LOVE they are about to learn that the first word WON'T was the relatively easy part.

Now that their personal transformations have begun with WON'T, they both have begun to face their fear of being alone and their longing for relationship and safety. They each now face the black yawning abyss of: ***Who am I? What am I going to do with my life?***

WILL

The Purer Conscious Knowledge of What I WILL Do in the Local Material World.

Introduction

You continue your transformation with WILL, your second major developmental phase, and as you put it in place you have no further need of should, must, have to, can't, hope, I don't know, I don't remember.

WON'T has let go of fear and worry, said goodbye to all unnecessary stuff, poisonous bitterness, grievances and lingering grief.

Now with the accessing of WILL power, you face infinite possibilities.

At first this will seem overwhelming and the danger of being blinded by your vision is ever present. Remember, in a healthy measure this danger is a best friend and solidifies the interdependence of WON'T and WILL.

The phrase I WILL gives you permission to start your life with your perceptions transformed and to actualize as you answer the questions of who you are and what you are at the same time.

The strength and depth of your actuality is found in effective WILL activity carried out in LOVE.

The challenge of WILL is to be impeccable within rigid bounds; it is not a strategy, it is a way of living magnificently in full awareness of the true poverty but unlimited scope of your resources.

WILL brings you face-to-face with enormous power. You **see** your untrue-self as in a mirror, freeing your true self of the bramble bushes of irrational assumptions, perceptions and fears.

WILL stands up to illusions while wrestling self-importance, self-denigration, self-destruction, self-pity and remaining fear to the ground.

You yearn in WILL, in the central nature of your true self, only for truth and reality. You can only be miserable by staying in your untrue-self created, fantastical universe of horror.

The laws of nature and man, while at times seeming to hurt you and hold you back, are, on the one hand, the solid ground that makes your walking possible and, on the other hand, the chains and locks that make the keys of your personal WON'T of such extreme importance.

WILL is aware of traps of worry. You watch your thoughts, feelings and reactions: fear, shame, guilt, anger, jealousy, envy, apathy, pride and competitiveness arise over and over again.

You are coming into your fully aware true self, your mind becoming aware of itself. You become aware of your reactions and let them go as you **see** that whatever impedes is another set of circumstances for your learning.

WILL is very quiet and unnoticeable; it is the belly of your true self. As soon as you accept WILL you validate your past and are free of it at the same time, except for what it is, a remarkable ongoing source of unlimited learning.

WILL lowers your head and stops you when you are up against huge odds, leading you to deep humility and gratitude where all must start, at the source, in LOVE.

Watch so as to develop mastery. Command yourself not to worry at the pinnacles of doubt or in the throws of a seemingly irreversible defeat by simply going back and resting in WON'T.

Total freedom is frightening and dangerous and it takes courage not to back away from its irresistible energy and the accompanying one hundred percent personal responsibility for who you are and what you do.

Now close your eyes and imagine the word WON'T in the center of your mind.

Now picture the word, WILL.

Now imagine them coming together, in truth, in one word: LOVE.

Picture the word LOVE in the center of your mind, hold it there.

Now open your eyes.

Watch how your world is beginning to change shape and dimension, everything flowing, infinite with potential.

The Principles of WILL

☐ I WILL is yes I can.

☐ I WILL is goodbye to internal criticism, worry, fear and doubt

☐ I WILL is infinite possibility.

☐ I WILL is transformation into anything and everything.

☐ I WILL is freedom from both the fear and hope of the future.

☐ I WILL is aim and purpose.

☐ I WILL is true surrender, not ceasing to make plans or take action.

☐ I WILL is **seeing** and **knowing** the light of eternity.

☐ I WILL is elevated awareness acquired through relinquishing attachment to stuff.

☐ I WILL is necessary detachment, pausing, reassessing, and considering all possibilities.

☐ I WILL is a process free of apathy and desire, open to higher levels of consciousness, willingness, neutrality and courage.

☐ I WILL is the least effort motivated by the highest purpose, to love the world in the bliss of LOVE.

As these 12 aspects of WILL become centered in your consciousness with full awareness, you begin the giant steps to I WILL be healthy, I WILL be successful, I WILL be free of suffering and then to approach the truth in I WILL love.

The SOURCE and PROCESS of WILL

LOVE is the source of WILL, infusing it to transform the corruption of power, vision and sexuality. To go from where you are to where you want to be, knowing you are already there, is the empowerment of WILL.

WILL and Awareness

The intent of WILL is a basis of and precedes creation. You are what your deepest WILL is and, as is your WILL, so is your deed and, as is your deed, so is your destiny.

The more your WILL is focused the more universal consciousness creates manifesting patterns in the world. Now, by imagining, and then saying I WILL, you break out of the mundane and co-create what previously had not seemed possible.

As you save up sufficient energy to accept this remarkable gift of freedom all that is required is one thought expressing your WILL to open the door of joy to celestial, eternal light. In this radiant light you actualize with complete confidence.

The miraculous nature of your WILL is a shift of worlds moving into your presence.

The goal of all your action is now **contemplation, knowing** and **being** rather than seeking and becoming. You slowly realize in the blinding force of WILL that, not only can I do nothing, there is nothing to do!

WILL and WON'T

The power is miraculously in these energetic words planted in your every cell. WILL blossoms life while WON'T withers anti-life.

In WON'T and in WILL you have established the appearance and foundation of freedom, cracking the shell of your untrue-self. Your true self emerges into well-being and the truth of LOVE.

You **see** and **know** that if your appearance and foundation are independent of the truth of LOVE you have forsaken your WILL and chosen misery.

Reading this testament you took a stand in your life with WON'T and now with WILL you hone the very quality of your inner and outer attention and intention. Your whole dignity and responsibility is realized in the strength of WILL. Now you stand by your words meticulously and impeccably.

When you get lost again in narrow focus, you contract with shivering fear into WON'T, before you expand again into the freedom of WILL. You **see** that fortuitous occurrences, accidents and coincidences are beckoned by your WILL. You have stored up enough energy from WON'T and the vast resources of WILL to be ready to enter the bliss of the third phrase.

WILL and the Past

In your WILL the anarchy and false power of your untrue-self is permitted and witnessed. Your true self can watch this now, wise to the temptations of past addictive traps and tendencies.

You clean out wounds of past pain and stop new pain with WON'T. This clears a fresh site for WILL to freely unfold its incredible energy. Now you **see** through WILL that you are not your disease or your pain. You WON'T be categorized. You have chosen happiness.

Consciously no one wants to be miserable, but untrue-self unconscious patterns have a different goal and they need to be carefully witnessed in all realms of sensation, feeling and thought. Their modus operandi is to scare you about change, to frighten you about the enormous power at your disposal, the incredible opportunity to feel orgastically alive in every moment.

Now you **see** your own previously crippling roles and scripts and through your WILL you rewrite, edit and change them.

WILL in Society

WILL includes healthy competition. What you WILL is often what others WILL.

You welcome the WILL of others with full awareness of the temptation to separation wherein the good becomes what you want, and the bad is any obstruction to your purpose. This is the addictive social trap of seeking and then identifying with competitive pleasure and the avoidance of pain.

Suffering comes when the wishes of your individual untrue-self to obey the group are in conflict with the personal law of WON'T that guides you into the freedom and danger of WILL.

WILL is aware of the rules and laws laid down inside you by others and the external, invented rules and laws of the group. As you evolve and transform in WILL you become aware that the fulfillment of any law is not a goal of the law.

Success in conforming to laws, literally and metaphorically, makes you an instrument of others, but when held inside, the laws become an integral part of the spiritual, as you are one with others. Moral judgments, however, that don't yield to experience and human heartedness are parasites that devour you with indifference and undermine your WILL.

The Process of WILL

The process of WILL energy is released by aligning with WON'T energy and then guiding this finite energy through your new unalterable intent. This powerful WILL intent is the source of internal quiet and strength needed to shift your fixed thought patterns and internal assumption sets.

WILL you now **see** is a precious petal of LOVE; in coordination with all WILLS it perfectly matches the needs of the world. Now you have purpose, as your WILL is the supreme wish of the universe, strengthening again and again as you melt backwards from whence you came, into LOVE.

When your WILL is to create joy and fulfillment by your action then your WILL, together with surrender, orchestrates its own fulfillment. Your attention creates energy and your WILL transforms that energy into intent.

Your life is now effortless and passionate, competent and free, a form of non-work, a form of play, but not in the sense of meaningless activity. You eat freely at the banquet and expense of other life. You accept your limitations. You **see** you are also a banquet for all.

Deeply in the process of WILL you recognize the illusion of gaining something in the future and the delusion of urgent necessity to go on and on until you get it. You sense now that something unknown is doing you don't know what. The universe is both a real and magical illusion, a fabulous game.

The game is a working game as long as the miracle of life is winning but does not win, and the miracle of death is losing but is never lost. You **see** clearly there is no separate you to get something out of life, as if it were a bank to be robbed.

As there is no time like the present, there is never anything to be gained, the zest of life simply to play in a field of LOVE. Rejecting knowledge and wisdom you seek no result. At the same time you are alert with clear intent to pursue specific knowledge and wisdom as opportunities for growth and change appear.

The sum total of the universe and its infinite possibilities joins destiny and all that is required is an attitude of gratitude, forgiveness and humility for WILL to manifest.

What happens now happens by itself, directed by your intent and surrender, your wishes and desires conflict with your WILL only until you **see** your greater creative WILL and **know** a truth that is your own.

The whole world changes as you are ready. You are pulled where you want to go. You are where you are supposed to be. You find your risk in order to find yourself.

You give up the familiar you used to cling to when it no longer serves you.

Your WILL, derived from the belly of your imagination, an essence of who you are, insists you can be different and transform beyond ruts and routines.

You stand on the edge of a frightening abyss of inner dread. You are faced with the choice of happiness and freedom, or being something, and choosing the comfort of misery.

WON'T and WILL have now established the preparatory, healthy, dynamic, energetic balance in your life, setting the scene for transformation into AM.

THE PRACTICE OF WILL

1) Comfortable with saying I WON'T to yourself and using it each day you add I WILL to your morning and evening concentrations.

2) As with WON'T, aim to practice with one exercise phrase for five minutes twice a day, morning and night, until you have completed the I WILL exercise-phrases below.

3) There will again accrue to you the immediate benefit of calming and centering your mind. You will notice and feel the long-term benefit of storing up clarity, calmness and centeredness energy.

3) Breathe in I WILL, swallow I WILL, see I WILL, feel I WILL and let the sound of the words resonate, vibrate and develop rhythm as they sink deeply into your body, every cell energizing and in turn being energized.

4) Be careful with WILL, and watch for the development of false pride at what you are beginning to do.

5) Always keep in mind that getting stuck with WILL is frequently caused not by WILL absence but by the overbearing presence of more than two WILLS in your imagination at one time. Your untrue-self is tricky like a multi-headed snake: true self WILL chooses only one image at a time.

6) As you arise each day preparing for your exercise, sink into the peace of WILL reminding yourself that WILL may initially sound like grandiosity beyond your reach. This again will stimulate seeds of doubt in you and fear in those around you. They will in turn unconsciously be downloading doubt, guilt and anger on you in reality and in the images in your mind. They will be saying, you can't say the words I WILL, you can't even think the words I WILL. This kind of response again shows that those around you in reality, and in your mind, are still living unconscious, doubt, guilt, shame, envy and fear based lives.

7) WILL, no matter how lovingly said, is a direct affront to all unconsciousness again. It is the second invitation to wake up. Your acceptance and forgiveness of others is complete because you understand and accept the fact that everyone is doing their best from their own level of conscious development.

8) Your WILL knows you are waiting and it knows what you are waiting for. You feast your eyes on the awesome, terrifying, unlimited bounty of the world.

You **see** clearly what needs to be done, one thing at a time, in the present, in the timeless domain where change comes with little effort and without a great deal of doing.

9) Your life of WON'T and WILL has become helpful and cooperative. Finally, all that is required is your action to fulfill your intent and your intent to fulfill your destiny.

10) Keep in mind that WILL is not just saying yes to infinite possibilities, it is also watching, witnessing and saying yes to the world of LOVE.

11) Watching your thoughts and feelings in saying I WILL, you start to become aware of past patterns of grief, patterns of resentment, patterns of regret and mourning, for your later contemplation. You see these patterns trying to pull you back into unconsciousness.

12) You gently cast these anchors off and, letting go of doubt, you catch the gentle breeze of LOVE. Filled with well-being, you sail freely.

========================

WILL Exercises

Repeat your exercise, this time with WILL, five minutes in total, in the same comfortable chair, as free as possible from discomfort and distraction, but if necessary repeat it under any circumstances at any time.

Start your music and begin by sitting comfortably with your eyes closed.

Take a deep breath in and let it out slowly. Let your whole body relax and let out stress as you breath out.

Continue doing this for thirty seconds to center and calm your mind. Keeping your eyes closed begin your vital work with WILL.

Begin by directing your attention to saying I WILL and carefully focusing on your internal life. Repeat to yourself while breathing in, "I WILL" and breathing out, BE CALM. Count: One ".

Breathe in, "I WILL", breathe out, " BE CALM, two".

Breathe in, "I WILL", breathe out, "BE CALM, three".

Repeat this very slowly for ten sets.

When you reach ten focus back on your breathing and let all remaining stress flow out of your body and let the word LOVE fall back into the center of your mind.

Breathe in LOVE and imagine your whole body and mind filled with LOVE and well-being.

Open your eyes when your music stops.

You have begun to store up calmness and life energy. You return control of your mind to your true self by becoming clear about what you WILL do.

========================

WILL examples for daily practice

I WILL be truthful.

I WILL be kind.

I WILL be calm.

I WILL focus on strength.

I WILL be humble.

I WILL have endless patience.

I WILL be impeccable.

I WILL welcome the masculine and feminine in all.

I WILL protect myself at all times.

I WILL wipe my personal history cleanly away.

I WILL break all routines.

I WILL be open to all points of view without attaching to any.

I WILL keep my thoughts elevated to truth and beauty.

I WILL laugh at myself and see the humor in all.

I WILL let go of the idea I am alone.

I WILL be aware that any time I attach meaning to an action this is my interpretation.

I WILL be aware that unconquerable pessimism will overtake me.

I WILL accept the sadness in the world and snap out of it.

I WILL ---add the issue you are working on.

At this point are you ready to fall into miraculous transformation. Slowly, gloriously let yourself sink into
The THIRD WORD: AM.

DANNY AND SARAH

SARAH

Mrs. Sarah Quill has put on several pounds and looks radiant and healthy. There is a For Sale sign on her lawn and she is waiting for final clearance on the offer to sell.

Surprising Danny, she took the initiative in the divorce and is already dating Nathan, the very well known, and established, artist-neighbor from across the street. Immersed in her new relationship she decided it was time she changed her name back to Tenor.

Her oldest son angrily moved out to his father's, but after a big fight a few weeks later, he apologetically asked his mother if he could move back home. He willingly agreed to pay room and board, got a job and began talking about going to university.

Her middle son gave up drugs, got a part time job at the local animal shelter and went back to school. His grades, on his own initiative, began to improve.

Her youngest son found his first girlfriend. They are cute together and heavily into hip-hop music.

The new Sarah had a real scare when she discovered a lump in her right breast but faced her fear and, going quickly to her family doctor, had the suspicious lump removed. She somehow **knew** it wasn't malignant and she was right.

Danny, deeply despairing, came back on his hands and knees seeking reconciliation after he had been diagnosed with a life-threatening neuromuscular disease. Sarah, while empathetic, pushed back her guilt and said, "Sorry, no, I've moved on."

Sarah went on to complete her undergraduate work in record time. To her great joy, she was accepted into a prestigious Law School.

DANNY

Danny had always been terrified about his physical health. He had become preoccupied with the stress he was placing on his body in the confinement of working in a cubicle. After quitting his job in an initial burst of energy, he found he was shaking with anxiety. Finally he called up the courage to visit his family doctor. In the doctor's office he received the bad news he had feared. He had a serious neuromuscular disease.

After receiving the catastrophic news and then being rejected by Sarah, Danny tried to kill himself by hanging. Fortunately his oldest son heard the chair fall, found him in time and called an ambulance. Danny was admitted to a psychiatric ward where he met a psychiatrist with whom, after some rough interactions, he established a useful relationship.

His psychiatrist threw doubt on neuromuscular disease being a proper diagnosis. He told Danny, "you may or may not have neuromuscular disease, but most of all you have given into fear and dread." Danny remembered these words and went back to his practice with WON'T.

He was soon discharged from hospital having made arrangements to see Kate, a patient he had met on the ward, for coffee. When she agreed to meet him he began to think about his WILL and he felt an incredible surge of new confidence in his belly.

As Kate had suggested, the idea strongly grew in him that his disease might be in his mind not his neurons. He made up his mind to discuss this again with his new acquaintance. He liked her and her interesting ideas about his disease.

Kate had been very impressed with his work with WON'T and had made incredible changes in her own life with both WON'T and WILL. She had what her doctor called a psychotic breakdown. She disagreed violently with her doctor's diagnosis. She felt he made little sense and made no attempt to understand her, or her work in AM.

After many fights on the ward Kate ended up being thrown into seclusion. She was a very bright woman and it didn't escape her that she had been humiliated and treated like a bad little girl who had been sent to her room. Her awareness of her own behavior, however, stopped there. Kate was unable to see that there were inevitable consequences for trying to set a ward on fire.

When Kate refused medication she was discharged against medical advice. Danny had been the only one she had been able to talk to and he, perhaps mistakenly, had been very impressed with the way she stood up for herself.

*   *   *

When you consider the seeming magnitude of these transformations you are able to **see** the frightening power to be accessed in WILL to answer who and what you are.

You also see the treacherous dangers to be faced in approaching the miracle of death and then surrendering in the third word AM. You are preparing to welcome LOVE and well-being.

Perhaps again you see some parts of yourself.

AM

DANNY and SARAH

It seems there have been a few more changes in the life of Danny Quill and Sarah Tenor. Danny, when we last visited him was heading out on a coffee date with a woman named Kate he had met in the psychiatric hospital.

Sarah had rejected Danny's pleadings for reconciliation and, while beginning to date Nathan, her accomplished, artist neighbor, she had been accepted into Law School.

DANNY

Danny for the first time in his life met someone who was interested in ideas he had considered important but had held in the back of his mind. He previously had been scared to express his interest fearing it would make him seem weak. His uncle, a tribal elder, had often spoken of these ideas and, as a little boy they had incredibly resonated with Danny.

Danny had tentatively, in the past, asked Sarah to attend a sweat lodge ceremony on several occasions but she had derisively mocked him. Kate, to the contrary, talked freely about the importance of spiritual growth and how love in its essence is helping another person grow.

Danny found himself feeling something for another person he had never felt, an incredible scary sense of his whole self disappearing in someone else's eyes. What started out as a coffee date turned into three hours of listening and talking. He walked back to his bachelor apartment in a cloud, his hands trembling in a new way. Suddenly he was strangely certain his neuromuscular disease was no longer important.

Danny, who made a gigantic jump into WON'T, stumbled in WILL. He now finds himself again facing the excitement, anxiety and dread of WILL, this time at its most challenging. In opening himself to love, Danny faces the tremendous challenge posed by the energy and opportunity of AM.

SARAH

Meanwhile, with her two older boys having moved out, Sarah, alone with her youngest son, has found her life careening out of control.

Her boyfriend Nathan has just had a remarkably successful opening at a top gallery. Impressed by Nathan's intelligence and worldliness, Sarah, against her better judgment and under the influence of too much wine, has let Nathan talk her into exploring swinging with other couples.

Now in her third year of Law School, Sarah's grades have been slipping. She has missed more classes and assignments than she has completed. Nathan, in his charming and persuasive manner has convinced her she has a problem in letting go and being spontaneous.

To help her with this they did magic mushrooms followed a few days later by doing them again. That was when Nathan confessed he was still seeing his ex wife, a local family doctor. He was parasitically living off alimony payments. Instead of becoming more spontaneous Sarah found herself becoming more and more morbidly depressed.

A few days later, Sarah's youngest son, now sixteen, discovered Nathan in Sarah's bedroom with a young girl. Nathan asked for forgiveness and promised Sarah he would be true. Sarah, sickeningly, found herself forgiving him. Sarah was terrified of facing the prospect and shame of another failed relationship. Soon after, however, she was shocked out of her cocoon by discovering she had a sexually transmitted disease she could only have contracted from Nathan.

*   *   *

Without a firm WON'T Sarah's health is endangered again. She is in grave danger of letting her untrue-self WILL slip by letting herself be led down a path to an equally untrue AM.

AM

The Purest Consciousness of Who I AM in the Universe

Introduction

AM is hidden in the same manner your true self is hidden. Your untrue-self unconscious desire for power seduces you into believing it has meaning and is the object of your life.

This is the spiral path down and away from AM into suffering and absence, attack and defense, living in the past or future: "If I hadn't? If they hadn't? What if?" These are the bottomless, fear-filled, fathomless worlds of If.

The world, as something to be utilized or possessed by your untrue-self finds only AM misery. Pouring disinfectant, pesticide and herbicide on a world of enchantment is the untrue-self-foolish-cost of attempting, with obsessive, unconscious blindness, to control the material world.

This addictive untrue-self craving is propelled by the fear of death and the fear of loss of 'me'. AM, however, is not an independent being but a special action of the world in relation to other.

Your untrue-self sees cause and effect while AM **knows** unity without cause. Your untrue-self's clinging to the idea of independence makes this a critical but difficult idea to contemplate and accept.

When any part spurns the whole and tries to control it the great pull of the whole gives a violent wrench until the part is dust. If your untrue-self 'me' tries to take the universal, infinite force of LOVE for its own use, awareness is devoured, and with this unconsciousness comes untold suffering.

The secret of untrue-self uniqueness was its hiding place right in front of your eyes in your vanity, position, status and world name. Initially necessary for development, growth, survival and intimacy, the untrue-self-local-name-of-hiding at the same time creates life-threatening problems.

The untrue-self believes it has an unique point of view within the universal AM but thereby has created a restricted ability to imagine beyond its own narrow boundaries. This is the same untrue-self enclosing nothing.

But as your true self emerges with awesome power, and then submerges into LOVE, AM is experienced and the world changes from deception to joy and wonder. In the universal AM everything is not only possible it already exists and simply requires awareness to collapse it into reality in the local world.

The more you **see** yourself as AM, the more your true self emerges and merges into intimacy in LOVE. The more other is AM, the more a living, breathing gap is created between your untrue-self and AM. In this gap you **see** where true self awareness is living, or, being corrupted by untrue-self 'me' and 'mine.'

Everyone conspires to conceal unity and look as different as possible, but it is much more than an idea or belief that nothing exists except AM. This is a complete revolution and subversion of normal life revealing the beauty and truth of the miracles of life and death.

Self-importance and self-denigration are freely let go of to access the deep reality that in AM everything is an unfathomable mystery beyond realization. This is abject humility and frightening awe, **knowing** that you also are a mystery amongst the mystery.

Being part of the mystery, your untrue-self 'me' cannot and need not be gotten rid of. It can only be overcome through intense contemplation, because as winners need losers, your untrue-self needs and easily finds a life that amounts to something or a pathway to being someone, where, instead of you playing your part, your part plays you.

Roles of your untrue-self separate. AM timelessly and limitlessly unifies.

Your untrue-self needs approval. AM is immune to all attacking denigration and praising idealization whether from your untrue-self or other.

The power of the untrue-self has taken up its proper place when there is no more labeling or categorizing, no wearing masks and no putting yourself or others in a box.

In AM the untrue-self exists briefly, as necessary, willingly and meekly taking up its useful pragmatic role as a shiny, freshly-painted, surrounding surface.

Thought patterns, their power removed, are witnessed until, in patient contemplation, energetic thoughts arise and your integrated self **sees** the THREE WORDS. You close your eyes until WON'T, WILL and AM fill your mind and body and merge into LOVE.

You experience with realization and shock. Your mind is observing and witnessing itself at the center where spirit is AM and identity dissolves in one consciousness.

Now close your eyes and imagine the FIRST WORD WON'T in the center of your mind.

Now picture the SECOND WORD WILL.

Now picture the THIRD WORD AM and see how WON'T and WILL are welcomed and taken in gently.

Now imagine the THREE WORDS restfully leaning toward LOVE aroused and tingling with strength. Then see them coming together, in truth, in LOVE.

Picture the word LOVE in the center of your mind and hold it there lightly.

Open your eyes.

Free in action, fully aware of the birth pangs of the THREE WORD fusion into LOVE, you watch how your world is changing shape and dimension, everything flowing, infinite with potential.

Now dawns the brightest day. AM sinks into well-being not by self-denial and the slightest sacrifice but by carrying the THREE WORDS outward in LOVE.

The Principles of AM

☐ AM is here and now.

☐ AM is receiving and giving energetic love.

☐ AM is experiencing freedom and meaning.

☐ AM is freedom from grasping, ordering or dictating.

☐ AM is an entirely sane mystery transforming the untrue and true self into LOVE.

☐ AM is unity consciousness beyond time, unlimited, immune to attack and adulation.

☐ AM is always active, but most present when ordinary senses are still, so that contemplation begins.

☐ AM is a mirror of energy never found in the material world.

☐ AM is you exactly as you are, a focal point of the whole universe, an expressed incarnation of LOVE.

☐ AM is one with WON'T and WILL, free of desire, conflict and fear, immersed in the universal flow of LOVE.

☐ AM is love and compassion for every form and the world.

☐ AM is the miracle of life that is miraculous death.

As these 12 aspects of AM become your consciousness in full awareness, you **see** the awesome, frightening, beauty and truth of the magnificent world and sinking into well-being you surrender to LOVE.

The SOURCE and PROCESS of AM

LOVE is the source of AM, infusing it to transcend all planes of existence. To live in the blissful energetic light of unity consciousness is the empowerment of AM.

WON'T, WILL and AM

Your success in saying I WON'T and then I WILL means you are feeling new ease and peace of mind. Your mind is turning inward to know itself, inward to experience who and what you are and outward to the one mind in and surrounding you.

Being AM, you watch carefully for self-importance sneaking up. You stay carefully, but not obsessively, centered in WON'T and WILL.

WON'T you **see** is AM letting go. WILL you **see** is AM projected into the future with utter certainty, your second birth, wherein lies immortality and freedom.

Only when all speech has ceased within, when you simply flow between WON'T, WILL and AM do you live in LOVE.

Go back to WON'T carefully as needed. The temptation is strong to withdraw from the world, to find others as unworthy, annoying, unaware and on different planes. Anything or any other you reject you will later have to accept.

Great care must be taken, great self-discipline exercised. The closer you are to transformation the greater the danger of the traps of WON'T and WILL and of losing your mind in AM by not fully understanding that AM is only AM in relationship to the other.

This is incredibly frightening, orgasmically exciting, and you shiver with immense fear. *You flow in WON'T and WILL and AM.* You choose and create plans. Most around you still experience their life unconsciously happening to them, the difference being the choices not made.

AM in Society

Now on falling back into AM you collaborate and cooperate as a part of an harmonious, passionate system filled with local forms that are only knowable in relationship to AM. **Knowing** this is sanity and peace of mind.

All local things are simply figure/ground processes of unity, the outline of flesh and the inline of background. The features of a situation arise mutually, patterns in time and space. AM is the total social situation immersed in the universe of LOVE.

The parts of society fit into the whole but they don't compose a whole. The whole is a kaleidoscopic pattern of temporary, ever changing parts.

The worldly aspire to be everywhere while AM is nowhere. The worldly want to amount to something while AM is no thing embracing and dwelling inside but never had within.

You do not face life anymore, in AM you are in relationship to all. You gain nothing from awakening as AM, but there is more than you ever sought, an end in itself without purpose or goal. Things being what they are only in relation to other presence your self-importance dissolves in laughter.

Now every detail of the world is in order, perfectly interconnected so that nothing is irrelevant, nothing unessential. You are action and movement, the meaninglessness, transience and emptiness of the world filled with joy. You are free from demanding rewards from the outside world.

Now you discover the answer for once and for all to the question: Who am I? And the answer I AM centers you in the light, in the presence behind, in relationship to the other, as you grow in wisdom with less concern but more respect for the social group as a whole.

AM is an incredible, frightening leap to joy, perfect peace flowing over and through your total being as meditation becomes contemplation.

Seeing you are always only AM in relation to the other AM, you accept and allow yourself to be as you are. Spontaneity is now so free and harmonious it needs no control and requires no further conscious scrutiny.

Seeing into this nothingness, this timelessness, is desolation beyond suicide, despair that is the bliss of AM. You **see** and understand in complete disillusion that only when you become nothing do you become everything. You surrender to the unknowable AM and a suppressed feeling shoots upward, a fountain gushing with the purest joy.

The Process of AM

Alone in AM for long periods everything is simpler and comfort increases. Fully in AM, awareness is heightened and the external world of other is a perfectly focused projection of your internal world.

Thinking, talking about, or seeking AM, there is no AM to be found. AM is revealed, never discovered. To want AM is to lack AM.

As AM is experienced, the particular and the energetic flow of the universe that makes the particular possible is **seen**. AM directs WILL but, since AM has no desire, there is no longer actualization from need. Freed from past imprisonment in useless seeking and owning, there is no need to do anything

You reclaim your mind from anxiety and obsession by listening to the whispers of AM. You pay attention to your sensations and feelings and acknowledge the luminous images that appear. You feel the life and truth and well-being of AM in your body.

Serving AM includes all ways of living. Allowing your true self the freedom to love the world, you discover AM is not what you become but what you are in spite of yourself.

As you **see** and open to signs around you, you settle back into AM feeling loved and cared for by infinite intelligence. Amazing grace simply happens.

There is now a shifting, at times a shape shifting, as you realize you are in the universe and the universe is in you. You now **know** you have inner security free of anxiety as you have access to an infinite supply of everything.

Freedom comes from embracing the unknown in the deep wisdom of insecurity. Wisdom, compassion, forgiveness and playfulness are flow in AM.

You give up right or wrong and all defensiveness. Everything is honored and nothing matters. Problems are no longer who you are.

This **knowing** AM by unknowing is the pure spiritual state of being at one with your experience. When naming, labeling and construction are refused what is left is the life mystery you are creating. The mystery of life itself is a beam of light to be used and seen, but never caught, an unknowable something, the basis of what you now **know**: I AM.

Realization arrives like the dawn: You are beyond outer form. The whole knowledge of the universe is self-knowledge, self-awareness and the translation of external events into bodily processes.

Silently listening to the stillness in your core, the mind, not provable, is as invisible as AM. Stepping outside, you watch your thoughts.

At first there are sparks, and then a flood of light from inside and out, as you immerse in a process of pure awareness beyond your untrue-self. This is AM, where lower consciousness emotion melts away.

The startling wonder is that AM, no matter how inconceivable, simply and truly is. This realization leaves you with nothing but a choice: to laugh or cry.

Say it now, I AM, and watch a smile and then laughter arise. As nothing you are the still point of complete awareness.

Laugh until your untrue-self is about to die. Weep tears of joy. Let your untrue-self live in the humor and laughter that one thinks one is a creature in existence, not also of existence with others and everything else.

Join in the play knowing it is a play. You suffer only when you take seriously what was made for fun.

You become woman or man only when you lose your sense of levity. Found your life upon this comical, tragic, one-point, fathomless abyss. Free in innocence, perceptual experience is transformed into loving the world in awesome awareness.

As your laughter subsides, a true and boundless sadness, an oppressive sense of loss, a dreadful incompleteness comes over you that you WILL to snap out of, for sadness is a prison of guilt and anger, not freedom. Sadness has only one purpose: to make you laugh.

By looking out upon the world immersed in AM the universe looks at itself and laughs.

Creativity in AM

As you deal with awesome power at higher levels of consciousness, you remain aware of the temptation to misuse this gift of power. The level of creativity in which you are engaged makes it clear that all life is a miracle and, free from trying to understand itself, thought can think.

You see that all blocks and resistances to your creativity are inside. You have the central task of staying alert, open and sensitive to clues and cues from the universe, your mind joined with the one-mind field of AM in spiritual evolution and perfect trust.

What you think in AM is what you intend is what happens now with uncanny certainty. The lightening quick, unconscious solution of problems is your mind working in AM.

Coincidences and an opening up of opportunity occur with greater depth and frequency, while in surrender you trust the universe to bring the perfect outcome for you to grow and learn.

You **see** clearly now what needs to be done, that you are responsible for everything in your life including everything you think, feel and create. Total responsibility sets free total freedom.

You stay centered in the present. You **know** there is nothing you can't do. There is nowhere you can't go. And there is nothing you can't be. Yet you also **know** there is nothing to do, nowhere to go and nothing to be. You achieve frightening, dangerous perceptual clarity.

You are a luminous mystery in relationship to a mystery in which the entire universe with all its forms and phenomena arise and subside. As your consciousness elevates, you **see** AM in all things, your ability to fulfill your WILL directly proportional to centering in AM.

Setbacks are temporary as you stay away from self-indulgence and self-importance. You give up power and stuff in WILL and steady in WON'T you refuse to indulge in laziness or craziness.

But your struggle is arduous, because in AM you are innocent and as you let go and sink into LOVE you **see** the sly, unrelenting, snaky part of your untrue-self rise up erect again and tempt you into the warm, moist, insane delusion of guilt: You are a sinner!

With this temptation to regress and spiral downward into the delusion of sin, you make the choice to contract backwards safely to I WON'T hold onto guilt. You then confidently expand into I WILL forgive until the illumination and innocence of I AM perfect as I AM appears. Again and again you open up to the mutual orgasmic joy and ease of LOVE.

You go ahead with the ordinary, you do non-work and make decisions, but this is now ease. You do not ask what is the value of this new incredible feeling of peace for now purpose has been used to achieve purposelessness.

The last stronghold of false independence is a mere watcher or sufferer of all that goes on. The line between the watcher and everything that happens to you is imaginary.

When this line dissolves AM is not in a world, but as a world, and what takes place is neither automatic nor arbitrary. What happens just happens, and all happenings are perfectly creative and harmonious in LOVE.

AM in LOVE

You fall in LOVE where AM is lived in and experienced but never owned by thought. The LOVE of AM can be **known** only as lovers **know** each other, in the warm vagueness of immediate contact.

AM is being itself, not a being, there is no subject, no object, nothing to become. Your mind in AM is a magnificent tool in relationship to other, serving love greater than itself, no longer a survival mechanism attacking and defending against other minds.

AM is freedom in harmony, perfect ease in truth, perfect activity in joy and perfect union in LOVE. AM is wholeness rather than goodness, oneness with nature and other, unique, incomparable, individual, destruction-proof, small in appearance but great in reality.

There is no mediator between AM and LOVE. AM is information in the moment, the verb that gives presence and places existence where it always is, moving and changing in the infinite abundance and plentitude of LOVE.

In AM, all polarity, contradiction, and duality disappear. A varied and complex passerby changing every moment, AM waits patiently in LOVE. You give I AM to the world to lose I AM in well-being and LOVE.

Immersed in AM, existence is an action with the trees, cars, animals, government, and oceans. AM lets go of the myths of being a speck in a vast, enduring universe or a speck with a fabulous self who is evoking the whole universe.

Roots spiral down deep into the universal, purest consciousness of AM. In unity, in LOVE, lowly and meek where all meet in surrender, AM gains by letting go, spiraling back up to unimaginable heights.

You die in the miracle of your death to be born into life. You let go of your resistance to emptiness to find peace of mind.

You cease your escape from pain to free your self from suffering. You have fallen into LOVE from which blazes the universe.

Now as you feel LOVE in AM you are generous to others and increasingly creative. You write the story of your life profoundly aware that results are certain, yet plans unfold in mysterious ways. You WILLINGLY let go of outcome.

The truth being that, as AM falls into LOVE, in the bright light of innocence free of all contradiction, you reclaim I AM. You say I AM in LOVE and the world is unbroken truth.

THE PRACTICE OF AM

1) Comfortable now with WON'T and WILL you begin to sink into the practice of AM adding it to your morning and evening concentrations.

2) Practice again with one exercise phrase for five minutes twice a day, morning and night, until you have completed all the I AM exercise-phrases below.

3) There will again accrue to you immediate benefit and you will feel long-term gain from storing up clarity, calmness and centeredness energy. You are getting ready to excitedly live and willingly die. In AM you begin to die to the past and future and live in the moment, in LOVE.

4) Breathe in I AM, swallow I AM, see I AM, feel I AM and let the very sound of the words resonate, vibrate and develop rhythm as they submerge into your body, every cell in you energizing and in turn being energized.

5) Hold your breathing in awareness without trying to influence it, let go of all boundaries and feel life and light come into your body and leave it with each breath. Sense the fragility and fleeting nature of infinite and eternal life carried by the luminescent THREE WORD filaments of LOVE.

6) As you repeat I AM, hold your whole body in awareness letting yourself focus open and effortless attention on your inside and out, your breath moving in and out, receiving and giving.

Quietly repeat I AM again, being very present with your sensory experiences, smell, taste, touch, sound and vision. Practice self-control and self-discipline letting your experience move beyond all effortful control.

7) Let yourself feel the life energy in all your body parts, let energy roll through you feeling your whole bodily self as what it is, a field of immense energy and blissful exhilaration.

8) Now in AM watch yourself surrender, breathing in the light of new birth as you inhale 'I', and then watch the shrinking of your untrue-self, the shrinking of the world as a threat, free of all enemies, your physical and psychological forms softening as you exhale AM.

9) Living in AM you step out of time, for when AM becomes conscious of itself presence arises, being, **seeing** and **knowing** energetic LOVE essence.

10) With this new clarity comes an incredible sense of love and empowerment. When you say the words I AM and mean I AM there is no restriction. You accept the periods of tremendous confusion and doubt that face you and let their accompanying pain and distrust pass through.

11) The highest to which you can attain is wonder and awe. As AM creates wonder, be content, nothing higher can be given you, seek nothing further behind it, here is the limit, here is LOVE.

12) As you arise each day preparing for your exercise allow yourself to sink into the peace of AM by reminding yourself that with AM your exercises may initially sound new age and even silly. This again will stimulate deep seeds of doubt, guilt

and anger in those around you. They will in turn unconsciously be downloading doubt, guilt and anger on you in reality and in the images in your mind. They will be saying, you can't say the words I AM, you can't even think the words I AM. This kind of response again shows that those around you in reality, and in your mind, are still living unconscious, doubt, guilt, shame, envy and fear-based lives.

13) AM, no matter how lovingly said, is a direct affront to all unconsciousness. It is the third invitation to wake up. Your acceptance of others is complete because you know and accept that everyone is doing their best from their own level of conscious development.

14) Keep in mind that AM is saying yes to infinite possibilities. It is also watching, witnessing and saying yes to the world of LOVE.

15) Watching your thoughts and feelings in AM, you become aware of, and contemplate, past patterns of grief, patterns of resentment, patterns of regret and mourning. You see these patterns trying to pull you back into unconsciousness.

16) You gently cast these anchors off and, letting go of all fear, you catch the gentle breeze of LOVE, experience profound well-being and sail freely.

=========================

AM Exercises

Start your music and begin by sitting comfortably with your eyes closed.

Take a deep breath in and let it out slowly.

Let your whole body relax and let stress out as you exhale.

Continue doing this for thirty seconds.

Keeping your eyes closed, begin your vital work with AM.

Begin by directing your attention to saying I AM and focusing on your internal life.

Carefully, slowly repeat to your self while breathing in, "I AM" and breathing out, "perfect as I AM. Count: One."

Breathe in, "I AM" and breathe out, "perfect as I AM, two".

Breathe in, "I AM" and breathe out, "perfect as I AM, three".

Repeat this very slowly for ten sets.

When you reach ten focus back on your breathing and let all remaining stress flow out of your body.

Let the word LOVE fall back into the center of your mind.

Breathe in LOVE and imagine your whole body and mind filled with LOVE.

Open your eyes when your music stops.

You have begun to store up calmness, life and energy and return control of your mind to your integrated self by surrendering into AM.

===================

AM examples for daily practice

I AM innocent.

I AM forgiven.

I AM perfect.

I AM free.

I AM being.

I AM energy.

I AM rhythm.

I AM flow.

I AM awareness.

I AM mystery

I AM light.

I AM life.

I AM death.

I AM other.

I AM LOVE.

LOVE

LOVE: PERFECT UNITY

The Perfect Bliss of Being One in Spirit

DANNY AND SARAH

DANNY

Danny was realizing that Kate may have talked a good, helping another to grow, but now that he was living with her his life had become a living hell. She smoked marijuana continuously, kept poor personal hygiene and seemed only interested in his feeding her and continuously doing what she called making love.

Danny came home to find her in a near catatonic state saying, I am, over and over again. When he tried to talk to her she lunged out at him screaming, "You don't understand, you're like all the rest." Thrashing in front of him she howled, "I am, I am, you never cared about me."

Kate fell to the floor weeping and Danny kneeled over trying to comfort her. It was to no avail. She went on stuttering, "let's go to I am Danny, come with me to I am" and she started to pull at his clothes.

Danny pulled himself free, got up and called the hospital and arranged for the police to come to the house. Kate, now partly naked, sunk into an officer's arms seductively and, wrapped in a blanket, she was carried out of the flat, off to the hospital again, screaming, "I am, Danny, I am, I am."

This shook him up so much that Danny, not knowing what else to do, called Kate's spiritual advisor to tell him what had happened. Danny desperately needed to talk with somebody. This conversation led, with unexpected synchrony, to Danny mentioning his own concerns and the advisor agreeing to see him the next week.

Rightly apprehensive about this man's motivation in seeing him so quickly, but feeling desperate, Dan was anxious at the first visit. But, in this advisor, Danny found someone familiar with aboriginal healing who was able to review the power he had unleashed in WON'T and how he had got off track with I WILL. With this man's help he was able to access childhood memories of fishing and canoeing with his grandmother and his love of Nature. He came to understand how, in his passivity in his marriage, he had turned away from what he really loved.

The advisor asked him his grandmother's name and, as if hit by lightning, Danny looked up shaking his head and said, "Her name was Sarah." This led to Danny talking at length about his relationship with his grandmother and his amazement that she never seemed to age. Danny said he could see on the surface she was getting older but when he looked at her it was as if she was a newborn. The advisor looked away at that moment and told Danny that he had been blessed because his grandmother understood the force of LOVE. Danny didn't quite understand what the advisor was saying, but he felt something shift inside. He decided to visit his grandmother as soon as possible.

With the advisor's encouragement Danny began to explore the possibility of finding work near the water he loved. This led to him contacting a woman who was putting a sailing crew together for tourists to see the lakes. He was hired.

Many cruises later, sharing their love of the open water, Danny and the boat's owner, Paula, headed out on the lake again. They were beginning to fall in love.

She came from a mixed background with an absent, alcoholic father. She struggled with significant self-esteem problems.

Divorced once herself, she had vowed to never let herself become so dependent again. After separating from her husband, she had taken out the last of her savings, bought herself the boat she had always wanted and started her own, now promising business. She had just received her divorce papers when Danny arrived at the pier in response to her ad.

The wide-open lake provided a perfect opportunity for intimate discussion and Danny discussed the frightening, exhilarating work with AM that he had started with his advisor and his painful, still guilt-filled relationships with his past. They discussed the importance of returning to WON'T over and over again and how the THREE WORDS, like the tide, flowed back and forth with rhythm.

Paula, at first frightened by her attraction to Danny, was now completely enthralled by his openness. It was just nine months later rounding a jagged peninsula that someone had romantically named the Cape of Good Hope, that Danny, growing in love and respect with each passing day, proposed to Paula.

Paula had learned a great deal from her first marriage. She **saw** Danny clearly and had no doubt he was her completion. She gleefully accepted his proposal and they arranged to marry that fall.

Danny then brought up the idea of his boys attending the wedding and Paula eagerly nodded her assent. Danny picked up the phone.

SARAH

Sarah had not been inactive herself.

Her youngest son and his girlfriend had by now moved out and were living together. It was the two of them that had awakened her. They were both sitting on the old couch in her bedroom staring at her when she opened her eyes. With deep concern they had asked together, "What's the matter with you?"

It was at that moment that she thought about her psychiatrist and how he had helped her to get back on her feet. He had talked about her WILL and encouraged her to get a divorce and go back to school.

Suddenly terrified by the message she was sending to this young couple, she got up and hugged them both and said, "I've just been upset for awhile but now everything is going to be alright."

She led them downstairs and made them blueberry pancakes and bacon. The kitchen filled with warm, succulent aromas as they ate and chatted.

After the two of them had left Sarah thought, "I AM going to get myself back together". She phoned her psychiatrist who welcomed her and arranged an appointment.

Later in the psychiatrist's office, they discussed how a firm WON'T is the fundamental basis of WILL and with new insight she began again to reorder her life.

She sadly said goodbye to Nathan and with her psychiatrist's support arranged to meet with the Dean of the Law School. He turned out to be very understanding but firm. He explained to her that becoming anything was always very difficult and that you had to WILL to become something before you can find your self. It suddenly dawned on her what her psychiatrist had meant when he said WILL naturally leads to AM.

Sarah began to apply herself intensely to her studies. She became fascinated with how the Law was like a living evolving organism. She immersed herself in understanding how family law related to corporate law that in turn related to the very making of Law.

Sitting in the Law Library a week before graduation reading Aristotle's Aesthetics, she was suddenly overcome with at first a sensation and then a deep and peaceful feeling. She felt filled with light and the library itself began to illuminate. For the briefest moment she was overcome with the greatest joy, certain she was at one with the universe.

Graduating from Law School with honors, she committed herself to getting her life together before she entered another serious relationship. It wasn't long before she was headhunted by one of the biggest firms in her dream city. She took the articling job feeling it was answering some sort of call. Sarah felt deeply in her heart that this position was meant to be.

It was while preparing to move that she received a phone call from Danny. She was happy for him and happy to hear about his own work in AM. She was doubtful his plan for the boys would materialize but wished him good luck. She excitedly shared the fact she was moving to start her dream job.

For the first time in her life feeling she **knew** herself, her heart throbbing in her chest, her body warm and tingling at the sense of awareness of her life purpose, Sarah closed the door and headed for the cab to take her to the airport.

DANNY

Alienated from his sons since the marital break-up, Danny fearfully opened his heart and called them. As he dialed, he wondered aloud to Paula if they might be interested in attending a sweat-lodge ceremony too. There was no answer on any of his sons' lines so he left them each a message.

Danny stood on the bow of the boat with Paula standing beside him, the two of them facing the horizon, the breeze whistling through the sails, the moonlight shimmering on the water. He was overcome with waves of joy, encompassed by an oceanic feeling.

He quietly whispered in Paula's ear "I AM paradise because of you Paula. I love you Paula."

She held him tight against the mast and whispered back.

LOVE

LOVE is real. LOVE is every manifestation of reality. LOVE is the force of life. The unique result of directing your spirit inward towards itself is the beginning of the bliss of LOVE, extending love outward.

LOVE is one miracle, I AM, the finite, and at the same time two miracles, I AM LOVE, the infinite. LOVE is also a third miracle standing astride the two; and all suffering flies off with the falcon, gone forever into eternity, the bliss of LOVE the truth of all destiny: to love the world.

A multitude of colors appear before your eyes with a humming of joy so pure and clear that you experience them both inside and outside. You **know** that the sliver of difference between outside and inside is a slice of fear, the last barrier and resistance to well-being and letting go in LOVE.

Now the very transformation of objects and events is no longer a dream but a reality and a process you have become through your heightened awareness. The bliss you feel in your sense of incredible, calm, well-being is energetic light in your body. You have absolute certainty that what you ask for will be given.

Something is happening to you in what can only be called a state of amazing grace and you willingly welcome it. In utter vulnerability and complete defenselessness, you **see** that victimhood and sainthood are one, perpetrator and victim join as brothers and sisters.

All duality and opposites, the lion and the lamb, which began their coalescence in AM, are melded perfectly in LOVE. There are no words and no communication but being held in LOVE.

As LOVE your human race is over, all suffering is gone. You welcome all because the good is perfect atonement and the evil an illusion.

Your choice was always there, to love or live in a separate material world. Choosing the THREE WORDS is choosing the truth of LOVE and true perception. Now that you have made the choice your purpose is the peace of LOVE.

You are free to act, as the impulse moves you and the signs show you how to stay still and move at the same time. You do repetitions of THE THREE WORDS and take LOVE outward to know it as your own.

There is no love more difficult than this LOVE that calls you to be faithful to higher awareness. You are not here as a slave to yourself or the world, you are a lover.

The light of this LOVE is the transformed recognition that life is complete in each moment, whole and always renewing. This is to experience LOVE that is all, beyond need.

There is no further need to ask what shall I do to understand this, for to LOVE and understand are the same thing. Your freedom and fulfillment is in LOVE, another name for perfect comprehension in perfect contemplation leading to perfection of consciousness.

For LOVE is the ultimate meaning, the one truth and the joy at the root of creation. You have attained LOVE; this is infinite joy.

To LOVE, to have eternal life, means to know you are loved completely and unconditionally, and no one is experiencing the experience.

You have a direct line to infinite intelligence, an eternal source of energy, a source of light that penetrates all darkness and an experience and feeling of deepening gratitude.

With the gift of the THREE WORDS, barriers to LOVE evaporate, for these words don't gather bulk. Your thoughts lighten in their truth, as you recognize the magnificent purpose in the spirally ascending developmental phases of the THREE WORDS.

WON'T, WILL, and AM lead arduously but flow effortlessly into the highest as 'I' falls away. You let 'I' go and feel the perfect protection of WON'T, the incredible creativity of WILL, the experiential transcendence of AM and the absolute certainty that you are in LOVE beyond death.

This transcendent LOVE is bliss that turns the prizes of the world into waste and beside which earthly passions pale. To **know** true self bliss in your still mind is to undo all blocks to the awareness of the endless flow of LOVE.

Your light shines on the world, beautiful, undivided and whole. The ecstatic bliss of LOVE surrounds you with its staggering possibilities and results. Your self-importance gone, you strengthen in joy, joviality and lightheartedness.

As you no longer share the illusion of scarcity you pay complete attention to the inviting field of light, pulled towards it, light towards light. Paying attention in LOVE peace increases, for as you need love, LOVE needs AM.

LOVE is deep inside you, never to be lost, your ultimate purpose to enable the divine purpose of the world to unfold.

LOVE is the essential linked oneness of all reality where all drama, chaos and stress fade and disappear. Even in difficult situations, immersed in the life-giving energy of LOVE, nothing arises that isn't needed and nothing needs to be done.

Now without judgment the channels of LOVE bring divine intelligence to your world of miraculous adventure.

In LOVE is the equality of all. To LOVE one is to LOVE all, from the smallest to the greatest. In LOVE all boundaries are illusions. You are one and all is one.

LOVE is an event, a force between that does not cling or grasp. The highest perception of loving is the realization that you are part of LOVE.

To see LOVE in the present removes time and condemnation. LOVE is here today, time an illusion of past and future.

The light of LOVE exists for you to reach for it and feel peace and joy and **know** that you are home, immersed in LOVE forever. The gift you receive is your life in infinite LOVE. The gift you extend to LOVE is what you do with your life.

LOVE brings together and connects the acts of separation and union. LOVE welcomes all limitations and transcends them. LOVE is not to be earned, it is to be accepted with humility and gratitude and never measured against human merit.

As 'I' becomes nothing it simultaneously becomes everything. In the one process of LOVE, life is play and thoughts are energetic and light. You are certain of your eternal existence. You understand the miracle of death that is everything.

LOVE is in AM, only manifesting when you are convinced of the impossibility and frustration of trying to find it by WILL.

You have let go safely in AM and so you are buoyed by LOVE from which springs forth hope, awe, reverence and humor.

You are one self, illumined, innocent, whole and complete, taking charge of what only you can take charge of, an orgiastic world where everyone and everything is in LOVE.

Now you return to the beginning.

Close your eyes and see the word CALM in the center of your mind.

Let it fill your body and every cell.

Now open your eyes and **see** what you have always **known**.

LOVE, and with it well-being, is everywhere waiting, where it has always been and always will be forever.

Fall back gently and safely into the luminous THREE WORD filaments and LOVE the magical, mysterious and awesome world.

Now open the book at the start and begin to read again.

DANNY and SARAH

DANNY

Danny and Paula married and, to Danny's initial, great disappointment, his three sons did not attend. Their father's past for now would remain hidden.

As Danny kissed Paula, unbeknownst to his boys, far apart from him in space, surrounded by LOVE, they all shivered at exactly the same moment and energy began to soak into their hearts from their new roots.

That evening Paula sensed Danny's sadness and giving him a hug suggested he take the canoe out on the lake, **knowing** both the appeal and the healing power of the deep water.

Danny slid the canoe out into the shimmering mirror of glass, light pulsating in the tiny waves from the flickering stars, overcome with a profound sadness and filled with a deep love for his boys, Paula and the world.

SARAH

Sarah arrived in the big city filled with excitement and set herself up in a small walk-up flat near her work. She had decided to decorate with Zen simplicity but, to her surprise, as she headed out to shop for groceries she thought about nailing a mezuzah on her doorjamb. She laughed to herself as she thought about how the mezuza symbolized a powerful WON'T that previously she had not fully understood.

The city was vibrant and alive, teeming with life. The flashing lights, the cacophony of sounds, the smell and feel of fresh produce took Sarah up. The aroma of food cooking was everywhere.

The next morning Sarah walked between the massive skyscrapers trembling like a schoolgirl but filled with a new found confidence and certainty. She met and was warmly welcomed by her new colleagues.

That evening, as she walked out of the office building tower, she stopped and looked up at the sun reflecting and sinking in the huge panes of glass held safely in the intricate patterns of the stone walls.

Sarah stared at the patterns thinking about what held them all together and she was overcome with a feeling of love for the laws of the universe. She felt herself shrinking and expanding, sinking in grace and forgiveness, letting go of all regrets, her tired, whole body filling with energy, vibrant again, certain with knowledge, every cell conscious, filled with bliss and radiating love.

Sarah turned and walked towards her new home without resistance or anticipation, very slowly, pulsating, everything beautiful, everything true, intelligent, possible, matching her throbbing heart, slowing, slowing down. I AM she smiled beatifically, as she broke into a hop step laughing out loud, filled with joy.

AFTER WORDS: LOVE'S ESSENCE

ESSENCE and SCIENCE

In contemplating the ESSENCE OF LOVE it is important to fully acknowledge the remarkable and powerful contributions of science, the great teacher, to the well-being of mankind.

Science is largely about pragmatic, material and political usefulness and knowing the past to predict the future. It has shown repeatedly that, while its help to mankind has been and will continue to be immeasurable, it can also, as a worldview, be arbitrary and destructive. This creates a past of regret, anger and grief (Hiroshima) leading to an anxious fearing of the future (Global Warming).

Your untrue-self mind uses a similar but pseudo-scientific process for sorting and dividing things with identical seductive results, an example being the cancerous belief that a thing (your body for instance) actually exists in some permanent form. This kind of belief devours life energy separating you from reality and truth.

Truth about reality comes only through direct intuition, action and contemplation of experience in a field of LOVE. LOVE, as the teacher's teacher, transcends the scientific division of experience, being the truth and beauty of the unified present.

ESSENCE and SOCIETY

From earliest infancy on through the installation of rules, traditions, rituals, fairy tales and myths, by ordering freedom and persuading individuals to pull all-together-now, society creates illusions that are opposite to the illusions of science.

Social acceptance, as a social unit, is the lowest common denominator. It leads to ongoing confusion and non-participatory agreements where it feels like life is living you. Paradoxically, society's best interest is in the energy field of LOVE where sacrificial, good citizenship and distorted family values are not a prerequisite.

Your mind, no longer obsessed with what is socially good or bad has developed the heightened awareness that there is nothing more inhuman than human relationships based purely on morals. The great untrue-self pain is to be cut off, to be self-conscious, to feel unabsorbed by the community and the world. This leads to the addictive seeking of the false pleasure of pushing the world around or the suffering of feeling beaten up by the world.

The civilization game then, while also providing much, is a demand for loving behavior, living and being natural or sincere. Yet as soon as spontaneous behaviors are forced, they become contrived, phony and deplorable. This social, hypnotic state renders it difficult to **see** that life is a unified system of social, geological and biological co-operation.

In sum, the essence of your true self is not what scientists or sociologists purport. Your identity, your career, or your roles in institutions such as marriage are examples of the essence of the constructive and destructive aspects of your untrue-self.

Through the THREE WORDS you have learned how to fall back into unity, to attain the peace of atonement and to be present without separation. In a state of unclouded awareness you reject boredom and the functional, welcome the foreboding and the exultant, and purposefully cross from the material world into the energy field of LOVE.

Through the daily exercises and what follows, you are becoming highly aware of the problem of self-importance, its twin, self-denigration, and the power-drain of heavy physical, social and psychological attachments.

In these after words you will learn again to more fully accept the presence of, but renounce the power of, your untrue-self. Within the blissful freedom gained you will excitedly, and fearfully connect more deeply with the miraculous essence and empowerment of LOVE and in turn sink into peaceful well-being.

BODY AS LOVE ESSENCE

Your body is a juncture of and portal to LOVE.

You are a process of life and light temporarily housed in your body. This body/form is both an incredible instrument and a relationship of communication for your use and learning.

Your body is a symbol of what you thought you were. You are not a victim confined to it.

Your body, your mind, your untrue-self and its name-identity are all only real within created boundaries like the real but imaginary created ones that separate countries. You grow by learning how to transcend conflict within and across these imaginary lines and find well-being in the simplicity and freedom of LOVE.

Your body is always a true reflection of your mind and life circumstances. If you find conflict between your body and your mind your thoughts are lying. Your body never lies and conflict arises only when your mind sees itself in your body and confuses your body with itself.

Likewise all bodies are only named forms, the end points of a system of inseparable relationships not a juxtaposition of things. Underlying each body is a field of consciousness, the domain of spirit.

Transformation into spirit takes place through the access point of your body not away from it. Only by trusting your body and letting it go into the miracle of death do you blissfully flow into LOVE.

SENSATION AS LOVE ESSENCE

LOVE is the orgasmic sensation of pleasurable tingling in every cell of your body.

Sensations, feelings, thoughts and behavior cannot be separated or divided without cutting you off from your true self. You are your present experiences in unity with the world around you.

Tuning into these functions is the way to know your body's intelligent and harmonious responses and experience the source of LOVE and well-being in the silence and light. Self-deception about your senses is the work of your thoughts and imagination.

Feel your sensations without judgment, neither liking nor not liking them, without emoting about them. Whatever they are, whatever their intensity, whatever their feeling tone from pleasant to unpleasant, your sensations are innocent, the rhythm and ebb and flow of your life.

Even the deepest sensation of pain is yours to experience in the moment. Each sensation of pain offers you an incredible opportunity to see it transmute when you look very, very deeply into it and don't fight it, accepting it as your own.

Each sensation rushes like a stream or bubbles like a brook, converging in the flow of LOVE through the flesh that embraces you like the banks of a river. Focus on any sensation, go deeply into the experience of it and then let all sensations merge. Watch the waves of sensation energy dissipate and disperse, your body letting go of what it needs to and accepting whatever remains.

Then arises the accurate sense that in perfect peace your body includes the external world. You **see** that contacts and encounters are ends in themselves. To **know** each sensation in this way, as a whole and complete best friend, is to take your well-being into doing and into a state of grace.

EMOTION AS LOVE ESSENCE

LOVE is being aware of what you feel and accessing this energy to turn your mind and behavior away from the sensations of created internal drama to the stillness, creativity and joy of the THREE WORDS.

Emotion arises where your mind and body meet, your mind reflecting in your body, your body reflecting in your mind. Every emotion has its place in polar tension, deriving its color and meaning from its opposite.

The emotions that fill your body and mind, when allowed and felt, are a rhythmic-in-tune music, but if ignored, they become an out-of-time-out-of-tune-noise. As your emotions arise and whisper softly to your heart listen carefully to what they say.

Emotion moves from deep inside in the same way you feel how to move. Give your self up to the motion of your moods and the perfect rhythm of your emotional heart.

Let go of inner resistance to feelings you crave to suppress or dissipate in precipitate action. Observe your feelings from the inside without interference. They are a fascinating, subtly complex process of creation.

Discover the wisdom of your feelings by letting them complete their work in you. They are like your breath itself and being fully aware of them is a life or death decision.

Feelings have both problems and potential associated with them. For instance, the context of any feeling changes its interpretation depending on whether the circumstances are perceived as for or against you. What you feel is to an enormous and unsuspected degree dependent on what you think. In this way, you choose what you feel.

Seeking out feelings of pleasure, for instance, is almost always a response to, or as a result of, trying to get rid of or avoid, pain. You are almost always putting pleasure up against your own greater good and that of the world.

Go deeply into your pain harnessing its energy. Don't identify with it. Put the light of your consciousness on your pain so it no longer puffs up your untrue-self by pretending to be you. Watch the pain in your heart and accept it as a part of what is.

Reactions of pain to external events, when you don't remain aware and open to them, localize in your body. You are then magnifying and solidifying physical pain.

Glimpse the empowerment available to you in your pain by watching your resistances and attachment to it, the peculiar pleasure you get out of having it, making it the greatest pain ever. Watch your compulsion to think about your symptoms.

Go into your pain to release the energy your untrue-self is using to hide from your true self. In all attachment there is pain, and in letting go deliverance.

If you dwell in fear, grievances, or revenge, then you become unconscious, untrue-self pain. Listen to most of what others tell you and watch how they overtly and covertly whine and complain, as if they are not choosing what is and then refusing to accept it.

As you look at the world, there is always untrue-self opportunities to complain or feel sad. Just a glimpse at the seeming loneliness of eternity and infinity and the ongoing destructiveness and self-destructiveness of man can rock the thick, comforting bedclothes you pull around you. Snap your self out of it!

Fully conscious and shaking with fear **see** deeply into the peaceful emptiness of eternity. **See** your whole, empty, integrated self suspended in vibrating energy and well-being. Safely held by the THREE WORD filaments of LOVE, feel your emotions completely and let them do their work.

THOUGHT AS LOVE ESSSENCE

LOVE is a meeting of minds in complete awareness in one mind.

Every increase in awareness comes with a new definition of work: work that is internal. Not knowing this, most effort and suffering comes from struggling externally, ruled by internal, lower-consciousness, exaggerated desires and memories.

As long as you think or believe there is an escape from your internal world and what is, moment after moment, you will find no peace and freedom. Awareness, as pure energy vibration, is the center of thinking, a portal to LOVE.

Awareness transforms into energy and information. Energy and information become the physical world. Your mind is the process of observing. AM is the observer. Forms, you **see** are an energy field held together by the mysterious force of LOVE.

As you advance in your internal work through the THREE WORDS, you cross into an awesome reality where there are no boundaries and no need for them. Now you stop living mindlessly and automatically contemplate who is doing what and why. Now aware of negative thought processes you **see** they are resistances of your untrue-self mind to what is.

What you perceive is the interpretation of your mind, selecting and making the world you see. You see what you believe and, in your untrue-self, you automatically identify with these patterns of thought.

Your untrue-self mind strains from force of habit and it must be carefully watched. Instead of living fully, the untrue-self unconsciously chooses thoughts of security and safety, inevitably creating patterns of insecurity and fear.

These patterns are based on past experiences and change like a music player tuned to repeat randomly in response to external or internal stimuli. Fear energy feeds and waters the roots of these habitual thought patterns creating the false belief that this lower-awareness-internal-dialogue is in control of your life.

Identification with these thought patterns confuses you by leading to the belief you are your mind. This in turn creates the fearful and paranoid illusion you are separate from unity in LOVE.

Watch carefully for warning signs of unhappiness such as internal discussions around frustration, irritation, impatience, a somber mood, or a need for drama. All of these patterns are variations on themes of indulging self-pity like: poor me, boy am I stupid, boy am I ugly, boy am I fat, the world is unfair, I can't stand this job, and on and on.

Also watch for signs of self-grandiosity like: They are so stupid, what's wrong with them, learn how to drive will you, those (insert any group) are such idiots.

This kind of chatter, if allowed to go on, becomes a fixed way of life. These lower consciousness thoughts circle endlessly without solution because they, together with the lower consciousness feelings that feed them, are the problem.

If you believe this made-up play based on past illusions and fanciful fears you can just as easily direct a play based on reality and your real purpose: to access the hidden infinite source of creative thought and well-being waiting for you in LOVE.

In elevated awareness your consciousness is shifting to an attitude of open attention and contemplation, by watching the sensations and feelings in your body, by watching the thoughts in your mind, and in all circumstances by watching your behavioral reactions.

Seeing through the veneer of your untrue-self's enslaving thoughts, fantasies and dreams, you wake up. Contemplating the sexual, physical, psychological, cultural and spiritual motives beneath these experiences provides the perfect opportunity for learning. They pose questions to test and open your mind to the truth and beauty of unity in LOVE.

You understand now you can't force awareness. You let it be what it is. It requires you to do as little as possible or even nothing but to be the **knowing** of what you sense and feel and think, your mind a sophisticated transmitter and receiver in the universal mind.

It is important to remind yourself that imagination, intuition, memories, creativity and insight are only orchestrated through your brain. They arise from the silent, ever still, yet constantly moving, emotionless place at your core, at nothing that is, pure awareness, the present truth behind the illusion of everyday life, your undisturbed state of awareness, your perfect well-being, the bliss of LOVE.

BEHAVIOR AS LOVE ESSENCE

LOVE is choosing to live magnificently, focused completely on the beloved world.

Everything in your life is a result of past choices. Watching your choices you make them conscious but remain aware that behavior is not entirely based on thought through rational decision.

Temptations to behave against your true self automatically rise into your consciousness enticing you to indulge in taking an easy way. Much addictive behavior arises from the easy refusal to face and move through temptation.

Paradoxically this same temptation and its ensuing painful emotion hold the key to constructive behavior and freedom from addictive habits: habits that lead to a hitting bottom before you **see.**

The reality of seeking pleasure is that it leads to a state of being incapable of enjoyment at all. Examples are the side effects of the latest medical drug or alternative therapy promising you happiness, the hangover after drinking, the sinking despair from gambling, taking care of others and expecting gratitude, or, being creative and expecting applause.

Identifying with this victimhood is behaving in such a way that the past is more powerful than the present. Similarly, believing that what others do, or did, is responsible for what you do is a disguised easy way.

Accept that outside the made-up little local reality of your untrue-self you don't know what you are doing or what is going to happen in the next second; then in loving the world and behaving accordingly the force of LOVE is set free.

When you accept what is and **see** that good and bad behavior exist only in your mind, you find inner peace. As you transform your thinking and then your behavior, it becomes clear that there is no salvation through doing, possessing, or attaining.

But putting your attention and intent anywhere, on anything, you access energy and messages about your behavior. This creates specific opportunities and outcomes; coincidences with clear and useful meaning come into view.

So identify what is in your best interest and what is not. Organize your values so you are clear what your most important choices are.

Consciously and critically question your values not seeking approval or popularity. As you become aware of your behavioral choices, this awareness transmutes into energy.

In every situation only one behavioral choice makes you and those around you happy in the long run, even if the choice causes significant short-term pain. When you make a conscious, aware choice, ultimately all is nourished.

In a here and now situation often your action will be intuitively clear and incisive. Ordinary pain and stresses, however, are an opportunity to be, attend, and wait, until you gently **know** what to do.

Your calm contemplative behavior transforms both you and your surroundings. With this shift in awareness you **see** your behavioral choices, so fear and anxiety fall away and well-being arrives as a gift bestowed by LOVE. You stand in wonder observing the world as it is and as it unfolds through your conscious, value-based choices; and the purpose of the world is clear.

SEX AS LOVE ESSENCE

Sexual union in LOVE is an intoxicating, mystical experience, and a glimpse of life energizing presence in AM.

As male and female body/forms, the sense of incompleteness is great on the physical level and attraction to flesh is inevitable. It is important to distinguish the needs of your sexual/form identity from who you are as a being.

As a being you are perfect, complete, whole and innocent. It is beautiful if your body/form needs are met, but if these needs are met without love it not only doesn't make an essential positive difference to your inner state it is a turning away from AM.

If you separate sex from love you are seeking the end to duality on the level of body/form where it can't be found. Your physical urges are, in essence, spiritual: the longing for an end to duality, the deep desire to return to unity.

Equally, when sexuality is set apart in good or evil compartments of life, it no longer works in full relation to everything else. This is a paralyzing problem when it is the isolated area in which you attempt to transcend your self and to experience unity and spontaneity.

Contrary to transcendent sexual love, your fear brings about your greatest error: the inability to **see** the one you love and who loves you. Love of another as a thing or a part of a person is not love but the fear of LOVE. This fear can interrupt development and create a dualistic, dissociated, body-hating and matter-hating attitude to life.

It is fear that moves you into this violent separation of love and sex. You attack your love out of fear to avoid facing your own unconscious violence.

Sexuality, forced by fear, or aggression, into the pursuit of ecstasy, is expected to compensate for defective spontaneity and the stark absence of orgasmic feelings in other areas of life. It is then set apart from other experiences as the false but great delight, slowly sliding into further perversion, impotence, frigidity, or abstinent withdrawal.

If your love isn't central then there is no interactivity and no passion, your love becomes degraded to attain a hollow divided sexual feeling. The loss of passion, when sex and love become split, is the disappearance of LOVE.

When you let your untrue-self disconnect sex from love it is impossible to pull together your knowledge of WON'T, WILL and AM. Your relationship becomes distorted by the darkness of fear and the anxiety of your untrue-self grasping your love as a possession or as part of a person.

The unease in your body is sexuality's reminder that you are not fully in control of your body and therefore not fully in control of your life. Paradoxically, it is only by embracing this lack of control that you transcend life and death and return to a healthy sexuality and an effective semblance of control.

Both genders need time and a sense of peace in friendly surroundings in order to feel at ease and to connect and center sexuality with love. If as a male you fear your femininity, or visa versa, you can't be one gender in relation to another. If you are to relate to the other gender, or the same gender, there must be something of the other in you. It is in this sense that masculine impotence or female frigidity are emotional paralysis.

It follows that external or internal codes, rules, and laws that violate your inner desire for sexual love inevitably lead to a sinking into a listless, apathetic shrinking of AM and the ensuing depression of sexual desire in WILL.

Sexual orgasm, to the contrary, is the model for ultimate passion in the moment and in the fullness of eternity. Sexuality therefore is not repeating a familiar ecstasy prejudged by the expectation of what you already know, but a falling back into the memory of LOVE.

Your mounting excitement in the sexual is now accepted rather than grasped, a gift of awareness open to a complete experience of spontaneity and a full sensuality of feeling beyond gender. Fully alive in the here and now you nurture passionate touch. It takes you to bliss and brings you back directly into the real pleasure of being.

You let go of orgasm and the sensation of intense lust that immediately precedes it as a goal. Your resulting orgasm is not the sudden end of sexuality, but the bursting in upon you of peace and fulfilled tranquility in LOVE. Sexuality is the embodiment of the mystery of existence, not a drive to thoughtlessly manipulate.

In this most intense and dramatic way you surrender to whatever the process itself feels like doing. You come into relationship with AM outside your self. This sacred sphere of love with other stands above the social sphere because, as LOVE has no roles, every process is open and you **see** what happens of itself: lungs breathe together and hearts beat as one, letting your life come and go without grasping. You flow into each other with well-being and melting warmth, LOVE the third partner.

The glow of sexuality reveals energy heightening awareness creating real and divine life and then miraculously bestowing awareness in new life. Even without the creation of new life in the world, in passionate, sexual love new life is created in the world of spirit.

The promise of love and passion, modeled in the sexual, is the altering and elevating of your consciousness. Sex is, however, your teacher, a loving, spiritual guide to living passionately in all facets of your being.

Sex, then, is a vivid expression of your organic spontaneity, a positive and creative occasion of being transported beyond your conscious WILL. Your consciousness and sexual activity are the touchstones of divinity and by loving passionately you participate in and create divine union.

Here is the answer to what is real in your living experience and centrally what is real in your experience of love: In your emerging true self you have a concrete, vivid experience of the force of mystical LOVE, the sexual relationship of AM with another.

Between you and your lover there is the opportunity for personal growth and insight and a state of acceptance, never a trying to get something out of the other. This is love that is not contrived nor willfully provoked and not an escape from the habitual, empty feeling of an isolated untrue-self without another.

This is worship in which your partner is the incarnation of the divine and the contemplation of nature in its true state. You **see** that everything is not a metaphor for sex; Sex is a metaphor for everything.

Sexual energy is a life-bestowing source of energy to be treated with the greatest care and respect, not morally important, but important in terms of energy that needs to be saved and re-channeled.

When you are truly engaged with love for another then begins pure well-being, the extension of love to all. Every moment of love contains all the lovers and all the love in the world.

You have the wonderful sense of **seeing** and being **seen**. The only test of your love is that it has no ulterior motive, love or die no mere metaphor. You participate in the divine love affair as LOVE participates in the human love affair.

As lovers you are contemplating and exploring your spontaneous feelings without any preconceived idea of what they should be, but as they are. You no longer lead or follow. You advance and respond in synchronized movement. The psychological counterpart is your openness to thoughts just as they are.

You chose to be a lover because LOVE is a perception of the other that arouses in its wake a mystical, powerful emotion. You are able to **see**, intuit and sense the infinite, divine point of the beloved in the center of your life.

All your sexual ecstasy now has the quality of self-abandonment, of surrender to a force greater than the untrue-self, this is the rarest and most difficult aspect of your human

relationship: to unveil the flow of truth in thought between you and your lover.

The meeting of true-selves is a greater sexual intimacy than physical nakedness, the exploration of an ever-changing, ever-unknown partner, not an abstract role or person, not a set of conditioned reflexes imposed by society but a rejoicing in the truth. This is a position free from rule but not against it, a responsive entering into the full depth of your love's story, including her or his loves and triumphs, but especially her or his hurts, fears and vulnerabilities.

Sexual **seeing** is a window that opens to the waiting infinite perception of LOVE: the eyes of another. This love, contrary to folk wisdom, is not blind; it is **seeing** your lover with the accurate revelation of the eternal universe that is in AM.

Your untrue-self beliefs are strangled by two eager in oneness, embraced in love. Love brings the real, and not just the ideal vision of what the other is, because it is a shining of celestial light, a glimpse of what you are beyond your body.

Sexual love is LOVE'S natural soporific, anxiolytic, antidepressant and anti-insanity drug that does away with the need for untrue-self opiates.

When the socially right wells up painfully inside, stay at the center of sexual love, for your error is not sin and disobedience, but the potential violation of your well-being including your sexual well-being. In the end your only real error is a violation of the creative, passion of the life force, whose natural expression and outlet is your orgasmic well-being in boundary-breaking sexuality.

RELATIONSHIP AS LOVE ESSENCE

LOVE is AM in orgasmic relationship to other.

The quality of a relationship that attracts is a blossoming. The quality of a relationship that repels is a dying. Trusting the blossoming, slender THREE WORD filaments of LOVE is fully realized by the mutual giving and receiving of centrality and full commitment.

The other does not limit this LOVE. You feel both without bounds, both at once, the creation of a new, shared identity greater than either individual identity. There is no difference between your self and LOVE; the faintest glimmer of this truth immerses you in LOVE.

A relationship appears from a mystery and calls you from a mystery. It is the unfathomable, incomprehensible energetic force that brings lovers together in spirit, the purpose of which is relationship itself, a touching of the other with the breath of eternal life and LOVE.

As a lover you seek your own true self in the beloved, stepping back into the empty space in which there is room for the other and the relationship to unfold. You are born with a blank space waiting for someone to arrive.

You can't transform yourself or your love, you can only accept the space where transformation happens, and this is all you need to do. When you have accepted this non-doing in humility and gratitude and thereby co-created this space, LOVE and well-being enters like a stream of living water.

Chosen relationships, interchanging around healthy, shared values, offer the greatest potential to grow out of guilt or sacrifice into higher consciousness. While you previously couldn't conceive of love without sacrifice, now you understand that sacrifice entangled with guilt and other lower consciousness emotions is an attack not LOVE.

You recognize that excessive giving can be a sophisticated disguise of the untrue-self for the taking or giving of guilt and sacrifice. You keep in mind that friendship with your family of origin, as a value, can levy an exorbitant demand when based on lower consciousness emotions like guilt and shame.

You also recognize that while every actualized relationship is exclusive, others living in its light constantly threaten to break into it. Even a child that comes from this exclusivity will try to break into it. The child must forever be excluded from the couple in order to find AM in relationship to another.

When LOVE becomes the order, however, separation ends and unity consciousness begins. Derived as you are from relational process, the longing for relation is basic and actualization occurs through entering into relationship with other and/or the truth of LOVE. Indispensable and filled with deep satisfaction, it is an experience mixed with doubt and fear.

LOVE in a relationship, being altogether uncanny, shakes up your security. Whereas the material world stimulates, tempts, creates activity and knowledge, a relationship pulls you to the extremes and loosens well-tried structures.

Relationships don't cause pain they only bring out internal pain and unhappiness for illumination in LOVE. You are always faced with a situation that is the same as the one you haven't solved.

Relationship is always a cross-roads: one way tempts with the destructiveness of addiction and co-dependency, the other offers freedom and spiritual growth in LOVE, an exchange based on psychologically holding your love so that communication flows.

Seeking love or avoiding love to diminish pain is a certain method of increasing suffering. Seeking a relationship with your self is another way to increase your suffering because you are not two people. Dividing your self with anger and fear is the handing over of personal power to the controlling, destructive, untrue-self.

The depth of LOVE is frightening and not free of pain. It is therefore avoided by your untrue-self. For your untrue-self love is blind, as it does not see a whole person. Hating parts of others, it confuses the hated parts with the whole and thereby loses human-heartedness.

Another AM, deceptively, won't seem dangerous when your untrue-self behaves as if they are a category, or an experience, or someone to use. So if you covet the use of others, you are attached in addiction, an exchange based on untrue-selves.

In power relations the goal is triumph, conquest and domination. In your love relation the goal is different, to serve the energetic force-field of LOVE that holds all together.

When you are fully conscious you will not try to control the nature and direction of your love's growth, criticize or tell your love what to do. You will not label or attempt to change her or him.

You will spend no mental energy on being right or proving your love wrong. Patiently developing and storing up a boundless reservoir of energy you become a partner in illumination.

You sink into a loving presence that allows all things, and leaves your love alone to be, as he or she is, without blaming. You are the **knowing** and **seeing** rather than the reaction. You reciprocate love, rather than fleeing love in an effort to escape pain.

AM is the flow of circulating blood, yet a lover's gaze transforms it into the inhalation and exhalation of the spirit of LOVE. This creates the perception of the infinite and the divine in the other, an illuminating perception of the divinity in everyone and everything.

To love is to know that two does not exist, and yet each is fully autonomous, completely merged and totally inaccessible. You go to your love with your whole being in LOVE.

You carry LOVE to the world without boundaries, as you **see** that life can't be lived without the source that is greater than life itself: LOVE.

REALITY AS LOVE ESSENCE

LOVE is the force and face of reality.

The nature of reality is that your true self is limitless and transcendent. You are not at the mercy of the world. You are affected only by what you believe reality to be. But thought not connected to the infinite realm of consciousness quickly becomes insane, barren and destructive.

Subjective reality, thoughts, feelings, desires, imagination, memories and dreams, and objective reality, your physical body and the world around you, are not two realities they are one. Every decision you make is a choice that stems from what you think you are. And what you are is what you decide to be, both before and after the miracle of death.

You are in your mind and your mind is in you. It runs wild only when you try to confine, contain or control it. Reality as local cause and effect is an example of a controlling belief that both distorts and disturbs your mind.

Most people in lower awareness think that the so-called real world of cause and effect is difficult enough so they stay there. This misunderstanding about the nature of reality is what makes it so difficult for them.

Illusions about reality and others, for instance, are always illusions about your integrated self. What you see outside is a picture of your inward condition. It is always your interpretation that gives emotion to your untrue-self perceptions.

Whatever you pay attention to flourishes and everything you accept into your mind is perceived as real. This perception is simply a mirror of your mind, not reality.

Your untrue-self mind can be possessed by illusion but the true self mind serving spirit is eternally free, unbound, unlimited in strength and power, all reality emerging from the symbols of spirit: information.

Your mind is a kingdom and when you believe you are not ruling it you have given it the power to triumph over you. This is the untrue-self-reality of losing your mind.

All cravings of your mind seeking salvation and fulfillment in external things, in images of the past, or in the future, are a substitute for the joy of being spirit in the moment. Held by the force of LOVE, you and your mind continuously and rhythmically flicker in and out of existence.

FORGIVENESS AND GRATITUDE
AS LOVE ESSENCE

LOVE is timeless gratitude for, and forgiveness of, self and the world in the sacredness of each moment.

Your forgiveness and gratitude is taking back the power from your own untrue-self-mind. Freeing your mind of strife and conflict in this way you forgive each moment and allow it to be. You stop storing up pain, as no matter what happens, you **know** it is not personal.

Your forgiveness and gratitude means recognizing the insubstantiality of your past and your invulnerability in guiltlessness. A painful pattern means you have yet to forgive yourself or someone else. Forgiveness and gratitude transforms and removes all illusions

The alternative to forgiveness and gratitude is the judgment of a closed, narrow, untrue-self-mind. The strain of judging is painful and close to intolerable as it has no meaning and meaning gets lost because of it.

Only when you see qualities outside yourself do you judge. You invalidate others with your own feared defects.

When you withdraw blame from without but then turn it inward, it remains blame. Blaming yourself is, in fact, still blaming others. Judgment is the dark side of forgiveness and gratitude; and those you judge and don't forgive you fear.

Forgiveness is still and waits, it does not judge. It is your only sane response as to forgive is to be forgiven. There is no suffering that forgiveness can't heal, therefore forgive even the future.

Now go over and over the THREE WORDS when self-importance and self-denigration lead you to judge. With your forgiveness all suffering is over, anger makes no sense, attack is finished, madness ends and your fears are undone.

Recognize your innocence and the innocence of the world and realize in LOVE that there never was anything to forgive.

Interrupting the flow of time in gratitude, and trusting in forgiveness, the fragile THREE WORD filaments of LOVE perfectly support you in well-being and the world you **see** is LOVE.

AGE AS LOVE ESSENCE

Aging is the final frontier of oppression, the mistaken idea that LOVE does not transcend time and that wisdom is a consequence of maturity and experience.

The malignant idea of aging is a loss of wisdom and a loss of innocence, the self and other installed idea in the untrue-self that separateness and difference exist and are real, that you are your body.

Unaware that aging is the bedrock of all struggles for power and control, the untrue-self deteriorates at all levels from cell to psyche to society. When this idea is held tightly in lower consciousness untrue-self awareness is devoured by LOVE.

Aging is identification with the body: an untrue-self state of mind. Aging is therefore the corruption of LOVE'S gift: the time delay given for full awareness to manifest in unity consciousness.

The true self is ageless, emerging in joy and bliss through AM into the force field of LOVE. Full awareness in LOVE is the choice to **see** that the purpose of age is to mark time for the integrated self to develop full consciousness of ecstatic, orgasmic life in the moment.

While dragging the luggage of time prematurely ages your physical form, paradoxically, age is a glorious invitation into the pleasure of presence free of stuff and images of the past. Every moment spent in the present reconnects your being to play in timelessness wherein you are not pressed for time, or in a big hurry, every cell in your body nourished.

Seeing experience independent of form, ever fresh, ever-filled with the breath of life, born anew every moment, cracks the crust that appears old and burdened, exposing the miracle of death: the rebirth of AM, ever old and ever new.

Others feel your life flow and glimpse the possible as LOVE is taken outward. They see aging is of life but only its shadow and shell.

PAIN, DISABILITY and DEATH AS LOVE ESSENCE

Pain, disability and death are miraculous transformations of the finite into infinite LOVE.

Pains are your thoughts gone awry. They seek relief through avoidance and pleasure, until pain, converted into suffering, sinks you into degradation to help you learn.

By raising your consciousness through the THREE WORDS, you elect to change all thoughts that cause suffering. Your pain is a portal from the finite to the infinite and symbolizes the possibility of infinite perfection and the eternal unfolding of joy.

Your most important lesson is not that there is pain but how to turn it to joy by experiencing the boundless nature of LOVE. I AM in LOVE has no fear of pain, looking upon it as a dark cloud safely surrounding infinite light and joy.

Don't resist your pain, witness it, embrace it and don't label it. It is an opportunity to be reborn.

Don't let your untrue-self-mind create a victim identity and don't give into the urge to turn away from your pain. Watch your feelings but don't act on them, you are bringing light into the darkness. Sadness and longing are your keys to sobriety and kindness and their matching set, knowledge and wisdom.

It is as easy to feel no pain as it is to feel a great deal; but you cannot have well-being, complete and pain free without sadness and longing. When your mind turns inward to experience itself your switch for pain is mentally flicked off.

Pain is a feeling of finiteness not an end in itself. To meet pain and disability is to know it has no permanence and is an error in your daily life.

Your surrender to pain and disability doesn't transform what is, it transforms you and your world. Suffering is the giving of your life over to your untrue-self, your self-importance and self-denigration the motivating force behind your melancholia.

Pain is guaranteed but suffering is your choice. **Seeing** that you are the universe complete and one with all that is forever without end, ends suffering.

Your untrue-self is your problem not illness or disease. Illness is accepting your untrue-self blaming you or others.

Through the THREE WORDS, illness leads you back into LOVE and the opportunity to change suffering into higher consciousness. Illness is a life circumstance that has a past and future whereas presence in LOVE has temporary pain and disability but in its true self essence it is illness free and timeless.

A sickness label keeps a condition in place and empowers it so that it becomes a seemingly solid, untrue-self reality. Surrender not to the idea of illness, but to the reality that in the present pain and disability occur. Illness is an untrue-self idea that has nothing to do with who you are.

Your sickness is of the mind not the body. It is negative emotion in the mind, taken out on the body, a defense against the truth and well-being.

To the degree you have not let go of all outcome, self-importance and malice are still present. In this way you are still making yourself sick. To the contrary, as all guilt is let go and forgiveness and gratitude are fully present, sickness dissolves.

Through the THREE WORDS you sense a kinship with the universe, not only the sympathetic and beautiful but also the horrific and strange. These are the external embodiments of your natural awe, ghoulishness and creepiness at thoughts of pain, disability and death.

Your life you now understand is unity, life-death, dark-light. This knowledge alters your deeply embedded revulsion of pain and death. Now you freely feel the revulsion and the shame and laugh it away in the light of LOVE.

Your death is a return to the unknown inwardness out of which you were born, alive by the sacrifice of life. All life is convulsive and catastrophic, maintaining itself by slaying and eating life itself.

And so your pain and disability have an overwhelming dignity and reality and an awesome holiness. Sense the inevitability of your own death as well as the death of everyone you lay your eyes upon.

Now you see the loss of any particular AM is only rhythmic, energetic flow, a loss to the local material world, not understandable in words, but by the experience of the excruciating pleasure in separation, the beauty in the breakup, the pain and fear of union, the miracle of death.

Flesh, form and appearance come and go, but life **knows** the miracle of death translated into action, action with AM at the center, around which all else finds its proper place and from which you draw blessing, grace, gratitude and harmony with ease.

The shadows of death and decay are passing on and momentary just as the earth is born everyday, a life of endless beginnings. Your untrue-self is the inevitable constructive and destructive creation you live life in. Like a snakeskin, it must be witnessed and shed over and over again to find your true self.

In pain, disability, and death, your untrue-self can't play the roles that it has identified with, roles created by society to be predictable centers of action. It fears this shame of a dreaded loss of status. Even your need to be right is a fear of death, for if you think you are wrong you're mind-based untrue-self is threatened with annihilation: to be wrong is equal to dying.

But every pattern and form of the universe is temporary, and if you think you need more time you will get it. There is always pain, but the need for time and suffering are inseparable.

Meditate upon your dying form: die before you die. Look at a seed, at a flower, and learn how to live and die without living and dying becoming a problem.

Claim your life fully by passing in fear through the valley of the shadow. Seek out your hidden patterns and overcome them with love, gratitude and acceptance so you are not an unwitting tool wielded by your untrue-self fool.

Through the THREE WORDS you have woken up and **seen** this insanity for what it is. The death of any form, whether it is a thought form or a physical form, is only a tragedy when you forget its essence is LOVE.

Dying to the miracle of death is working to withdraw energy from reminiscences, desires and internal dialogues that become mind forms, so that pure consciousness awakens and strengthens in LOVE. You still create new forms and circumstances but now you are careful not to identify with them. You break all routines.

You understand and embrace the death of forms when you drop the illusion that life is a constant war against death and death is evil. You identify with the center of life and death itself, not with passing forms and phenomena. You no longer need to be in control of Nature, a self-appointed member of the top species.

Decisions you make, free of polarities like life-death, help you to **see** that detachment is harmony and the quest for permanency is a pure futility.

You do not begin to be alive in well-being until you release your anxious grasp upon everything, your reputation, your position, your life and your stuff. Hold onto your life only like grim death. Strip away all your stuff, talents, achievements and abilities, for it is only then that you can see death's miracle.

You can't have one without the all; you either keep all or let all go. Death is the end of illusion, the pure beauty and miracle of completion.

Abandon your desire for happiness separate from misery, pleasure apart from pain and life apart from death. What dies is not your consciousness but memory that recurs in every newborn as AM; to **see** this is to feel identity with all and to understand and live with gratitude, compassion and forgiveness. Now there is nowhere to go. Cross the narrow footbridge to your home.

As you cross over, Death, and her daughter, Fear, whisper in your ear. These are your infallible advisors, your true friends, the trusted truth-tellers who won't lie to you. The truth is whispered: Your self as a valuable physical body that lives and dies is the ultimate illusion. Suffering is yours, as long as you cling to it.

Death and the loss of everything is your fate and once you let go of everything, as you cross over, you have nothing to fear. You are alone, but to die alone is not to die in loneliness.

The last enemy standing is death. But death, in fact, has the least possible hold upon your mind. You are shockingly aware that this dark mirror reflecting light on your life is your best friend, the agent of renewal, as you shape-shift everyday.

Higher awareness found in the THREE WORDS never dies, just names, forms and illusions. You die at exactly the right time and you know in advance when that time is. Death only looks black, as the grass is green. And both are beautiful and true.

You were not born with the mark of sin. You have not fallen. There is nowhere to be restored. The force of death boosts your awareness, giving a higher value to life, until death is welcomed.

Your pain and disability opens a gap to surrender into the miracle of death. You fall back into seeming nothing and then

everything, what you thought was your worst, becomes your best: I AM death falling into LOVE.

Love to be alive celebrating the miracle of death. You have found your appearance before the world was made. In the THREE WORDS, WON'T, WILL and AM, you have found complete well-being and fallen into eternal LOVE.

* * *

Acknowledgments:

This testament has been deeply influenced by innumerable others. I am deeply grateful to the following authors: Wilfred Bion, Martin Buber, Richard Bucke, John Bowlby, Leonard Cohen, Joseph Campbell, Carlos Castaneda, Deepak Chopra, Sigmund Freud, Tich Nhat Hanh, David Healy, Pupil Jayakar, Immanuel Kant, Marc Gafni, James Grotstein, Louise Hay, Otto Kernberg, Melanie Klein, J. Krishnamurti, The Dalai Lama, Ronald Laing, Rumi, Thomas Szasz, Rabindranath Tagore, Eckhart Tolle, Swami Nikhilanada, Alan Watts and Donald Winnicott.

About the author:

Clark Falconer is a published author, an award-winning, former professor of psychiatry, and a practicing clinician. He lives and works in Vancouver, Canada.